THE MODERNITY OF MILTON

THE UNIVERSITY OF CHICAGO PRESS
CHICAGO, ILLINOIS
—

THE BAKER & TAYLOR COMPANY
NEW YORK

THE MACMILLAN COMPANY OF CANADA, LIMITED
TORONTO

THE CAMBRIDGE UNIVERSITY PRESS
LONDON

THE MARUZEN-KABUSHIKI-KAISHA
TOKYO, OSAKA, KYOTO, FUKUOKA, SENDAI

THE COMMERCIAL PRESS, LIMITED
SHANGHAI

THE MODERNITY OF MILTON

A Theological and Philosophical Interpretation

By

MARTIN A. LARSON, Ph.D.

Assistant Professor of English
University of Idaho

THE UNIVERSITY OF CHICAGO PRESS
CHICAGO, ILLINOIS

To

JAMES HOLLY HANFORD

I RESPECTFULLY
DEDICATE THIS BOOK, IN
ACKNOWLEDGMENT OF THE UNCEAS-
ING AID, SYMPATHY, AND FRIENDSHIP WHICH
HE HAS VOUCHSAFED ME

PREFACE

The Modernity of Milton is intended to fill the need I first felt when, as an undergraduate, I read *Paradise Lost*. I had, however, perused and partially comprehended this poem several years before that. But it was impossible for me to get beneath the surface of it, because much of what constitutes its content must necessarily be interpreted.

The point of view in the present book is that the vital thing in Milton is neither pretty imagery nor mere organ music; it assumes that the essential Milton can be comprehended and appreciated only by one who has some knowledge of his theological and philosophical thought, that is, by one who interests himself in what was most significant to the poet himself. In this criticism, it is unnecessary to deal extensively with source material; and quotations to present the author's thought —never to illustrate his style—will be frequent but brief. Those who have read Milton carefully will be able to judge whether the following interpretation is accurate and recondite; and this statement is especially true of such students as have, in addition, some knowledge of historical Christianity. To the reader or teacher of literature who is already familiar with *Paradise Lost*, *Paradise Regained*, and *Samson Agonistes*, or even with *Paradise Lost* alone, the present work may prove a valuable aid, as medieval theology and Renaissance meta-physics are now not generally understood.

To me it seems most encouraging that Milton has, of late years, more and more come to be regarded as a poet of ideas and as a man who looked forward. Such works as Denis Saurat's *La Pensée de Milton* and *Milton, Man and Thinker*—with which we might mention many brief-er ones by other authors—are immeasurably superior to such frivolous criticism of Milton as we find in Taine's *L'Histoire de la Littérature Anglaise.* And I trust that *The Modernity of Milton* may prove both an addition and an incentive to the new criticism and understanding of a great and sincere man, who was, first, an emanci-pated student of the past; second, a last exponent of the Renaissance and a partial expressor of Puritanism; and, third, the herald of an age that was just about to dawn.

It gives me pleasure to acknowledge the valuable suggestions and criticisms which Professor O. J. Camp-bell and Dean A. H. Lloyd of the University of Michi-gan and President A. H. Upham of the University of Idaho have kindly given me.

MARTIN A. LARSON

MOSCOW, IDAHO
February 7, 1927

CONTENTS

He died,
Who was the sire of an immortal strain,
Blind, old, and lonely, when his country's pride,
The priest, the slave, and the liberticide,
Trampled and mocked with many a loathèd rite
Of lust and blood; he went, unterrified,
Into the gulph of death; but his clear Sprite
Yet reigns o'er earth; the third among the sons of light.

—SHELLEY

CHAPTER I

THE RELIGIOUS BACKGROUND FOR MILTON'S THOUGHT

Milton's life came just after the pagan and during the Puritan Renaissance. This rebirth of the old and dormant religion was parallel with the pagan Renaissance; in both movements, England was a century and more behind continental Europe. As soon as one great human force works itself out, its opposite begins to gain ascendance; as soon as the movement in which Leonardo da Vinci, Columbus, Bruno, Paracelsus, Shakespeare, and Bacon were prominent had ceased to make men enthusiastic, another came which directed their vision away from the present to a future life. Such men as Luther, Calvin, Zwingli, Peter Martyr, Knox, Prynne, Cheynell, and Bunyan were great and unreserved exponents of recrudescent medieval Christianity. And Milton's greatest works are inspired, or at least tremendously modified, by this philosophy of life. Yet he may, only after many and complex reservations, be called a historical Christian.

We must realize that the Reformation and Puritanism did not seek to create anything new in religion, but sought only to strip from the church all the abuses which had grown up about it during many centuries and which had destroyed its spiritual efficacy. Luther and Calvin

wished to restore Christianity to its pristine purity—
that of the third and fourth centuries. They declared
papal and episcopal authority unfounded in scripture
and therefore null; they maintained the confessional, indulgences, penances, etc., to be monstrous abuses; they
affirmed that laymen should read and interpret the Bible
individually, and that they should have no intercessor
except Christ between God and themselves; Purgatory,
they asseverated, was a myth growing out of the base
cupidity of worldly priests; and, most important from
the doctrinal point of view, they declared the doctrine of
the Real Presence to be false. In general, the Reformers
—who were tremendously in earnest—stripped away the
ceremonies, outward performances of all kinds to obtain
salvation, and made religion, not a practice or an impos-
ing spectacle, but a life. To them, Christianity was, for
its own sake, infinitely more important than mere temporal life and death. The only death they feared was
that which is the result of sin, and of which the consequence is an eternity in hell-fire. But we must here realize that nearly everything which Luther or Knox condemned had come into existence after the fifth century;
nothing considered orthodox by Augustine was eschewed
by the Christian Renaissance. This great Father was
the oracle of the Reformation: his name is invoked far
more than any other throughout its literature. His
genius and vigor summed up and gave form to three
centuries of patristic thought; and he, far more than
any other, made the Christianity of Western Europe

what it has been during fifteen centuries. To know what he taught is to understand Martin Luther, John Bunyan, and Jonathan Edwards completely.

In many ways the seventeenth century was most crucial in the development toward modern life; it was the stormiest period in English history. Milton's whole existence is indissolubly involved with the great movements of his era. It was then that parliament fought the Stuarts to the bitter death and achieved the victory which conferred a free constitutional government upon the English-speaking race. It was then that the Baconian philosophy and scientific pursuits, which have quite revolutionized human existence, began to flourish.[1] It was then that prose was invented and prepared to become a universal vehicle for the easy expression of thought. It was then that the freedom of speech and press was duly recognized by law.[2] And, not least, it was this century which saw the hottest religious controversies and wars of English history; which produced a most violent reaction against all religion, piety, and conventional morality;[3] which saw the rise of Deism and the spread of Socinianism; and which paved the way toward such religion as we find today, without creeds, dog-

[1] Even Charles II, the gallant and merry debauchee, had his private chemical laboratory, where he spent much time doing experimental work.

[2] Cf. Macaulay, *History of England*, "Everyman Series," III, 327.

[3] I refer the reader to Restoration drama and to a study of Charles II's court.

mas, or, indeed, any vital two-world interest, a system not of theology but of ethics.

It is discernible that Milton's reaction to Puritanism was unique. During the days of its power, he was at war both with its principles and its adherents.[4] In maturity, he is said never to have gone to any church, and he regarded both the church and churchmen with peculiar hatred and contempt.[5] He allied himself with no party or organization, but he differed least from the extreme independents.[6] Until 1655, he was vitally interested in temporal problems only.[7] It was only when all his worldly hopes and ambitions had been crushed, and he retired from the sphere of action, a defeated man, that he turned to the philosophy of Puritanism for compensation and consolation; but even then he carried so much of his own Hellenic rationalism, self-assertiveness, and individualism into it that he transformed a philosophy of surrender and self-abnegation into one of victory and glorious exaltation. He breathed a spirit essentially modern into a conception of life which was nothing if not medieval.

[4] Cf. chap. ii, 73–74.

[5] Cf. "Lycidas," ll. 113–31. In 1832 Milton refused to join the church because he would have "to subscribe slave." He derided the learning of the clergy (*Prose Works* [Bohn ed.], III, 38; 83; *ibid.*, II, 77). He calls them "those indolent vermin" (*ibid.*, I, 277). Priests he calls the "consecrate [d] . . . . pests of the human race" (*ibid.*, 217). His denunciation of the bishops in his early tracts and his condemnation of the Presbyterians after 1644 are peculiarly fierce. But they are condemned, not on theological, but on political and ethical grounds.

[6] He belonged to the party of Cromwell.

[7] Cf. chap. iv.

As it will be necessary to use the words "Puritan" and "pagan" many times in the course of this study, it may be well to define them at the outset. We must realize that the conception of the Puritan which exists in the minds of most people is a mere figment of the imagination. The word "pagan" will be used in the ensuing pages to signify, not a historical period, but a particular attitude toward life. A twofold basis exists for the definitions here advanced: first the great documents expressing the attitude, the doctrines, and the interests of the Puritans on the one hand, and of the pagans on the other; second, the external histories of peoples where the one or the other philosophy of life has been dominant. For example, the works of such men as Athanasius, Jerome, Peter Martyr, Calvin, Whitgift, Bunyan, and Cotton Mather are in point as an expression of Puritan dogma and interest; and the history of miracles, of religious wars and persecutions, of the suppression of intellectual freedom, of the power of the medieval church, etc., are records of the external effects of belief in the Augustinian philosophy. On the other hand, the writings of such men as Homer, Sophocles, Zenophon, Herodotus, Plutarch, Erasmus, Browning, and Thoreau exemplify the pagan attitude as opposed to the Puritan or historically Christian. And the history of all art, colonization, expansion, physical and intellectual improvement or progress, secular philosophy, etc., are the direct results of pagan assumptions in regard to life.

Thus founded, the term "Puritan" signifies a convic-

tion of human sin, degradation, and absolute dependence on external forces; an abhorrence of all concrete or
sensuous loveliness; a repudiation of human activity and
a refuge in passive contemplation; a desire to escape
this life and to obtain entrance into heaven; an emphasis upon religious opinions and a contempt for ordinary
morality; an overwhelming fear of human reason; the
distinct realization of a personal God of justice and vengeance; and the mortification of all natural impulses—
that is, of the flesh. But the term "pagan" carries quite
other meaning: it implies a passionate love for all things
essentially human; an enthusiasm for every beauty per-
ceivable through the senses; a high degree of confidence in man's rational faculty; an eminent desire for
activity and intellectual progress in the here and now;
an indifference toward existence beyond the grave; an
ethic that is based upon a purely one-world philosophy;
and the belief that natural impulses are good.

We are unquestionably safe in saying that these two
forces have been fundamental in the development of
European thought. We may conveniently denominate
them "Hellenism" and "medieval or historical Christianity," the one-world and two-world principles of life.
Periclean Athens is the type of the former; and the Pil-
grims, the type of the latter. One seeks only that which it
considers good and excellent in the present life; the
other, looking upon the present existence as a short and
doleful transition from misery to happiness, a vale of
sorrow and a habitation of tears, seeks eternal bliss

in heaven.⌉ Of course, neither Hellenism nor medieval
Christianity is often to be found in an unmixed state:
the relative is frequent and the absolute rare. Yet the
forces, the *impulses,* are quite distinct; and it is most
certain that one of these was predominant in Europe
from 300 to 1200; and that the other is victorious now.
It is certain that the one was victorious in England in
1600 and the other in 1645, although there were many
Puritans at the earlier date and many Cavaliers at the
later. But even the most profligate or most learned of
the latter made no attack upon Christian *doctrines* or
dogmas. Milton belongs most distinctly with the Hel-
lenes.

Both, of course, are the result of great human experiences—experiences diametrically opposed to each other. They grow out of two sets of opposite but unarguable
assumptions concerning existence, both of which are absolutely true for those whose subjective needs they meet.
But the beliefs of the early Christians arising from such
needs were soon frozen into immutable dogmas and,
supported by cunning, tyranny, and persecution, were
forced upon countless millions for whom they contained
no subjective truth. Pagan beliefs, however, can never
be thus congealed because they can never serve as tools
for superstition and tyranny. Hellenism grows out of
victory, joy, pleasure, and exultant achievement. It
loves the present world because it is full both of satisfaction and of unrealized ambitions which lure men on to
the expenditure of effort: its ideal is accomplishment

and the enjoyment of success. Augustinianism, on the contrary, grows out of defeat, misery, and obvious failure. It abhors the present world because it is full of anguish and desolation and because it can offer nothing whatever to kindle man's hope or desire. Its ideal is transferred to another world in which all things are as excellent as they are here depraved and worthless.

The reader must not confuse "Augustinianism" or "historical Christianity" too completely with what is to be found in the Bible. We are not concerned with that; we are dealing with what developed from it. Nevertheless, it is infallibly certain that, given the condition of Roman civilization during the spread of Christianity and the enemies which it was compelled to overcome during its early stages, the Fathers could not have interpreted scripture in any detail otherwise than as they did. Great movements develop as they do in obedience to inexorable law. It is even true that, although Stoicism and Christianity are diametrically opposed in essence, we may find much in Marcus Aurelius that sounds like certain passages in the Bible, although these were without significance in gaining proselytes. A large view, however, considers always the fundamental and the historical as the truly significant.

Furthermore, we must not confuse the present-day churches (especially the larger Protestant institutions) with those headed by Augustine or Edwards. During the last 350 years, the religious evolution has been so great and so rapid that little of what was almost universal in

1550 is now to be discerned at all, except some phrases and forms which have lost nearly all their original significance and which are now understood only by scholars. So much of what I here call, for the sake of convenience, the "Hellenic," "pagan," or "one-world philosophy" has been carried into the medieval Christian that little remains of the latter but the mere name. The breakdown of the Augustinian philosophy—in which the cessation of open persecution was perhaps the most signal step—began in the twelfth century but is not yet complete. Nominalism was the earliest philosophical statement of the attitude which resulted in "modernity."

To try to explain Milton's relation to religious thought in Europe would be idle, without first explaining in some detail what Hellenism and Augustinianism are as philosophies of life. This, then, must now be done.

"Hellenism," in the first place, is the one-world theory of life. It recognizes no life hereafter, or only one so shadowy as to inspire little anticipation or terror. Its interest is in the here and now. Among the Greeks, the gods were only magnified and immortal men; their favor was invoked only that they might confer some temporal and material benefit: they had no control over the future life. Thus, Greek religion could not be even as important as the joys and sorrows of daily life. The Hebrew God was the god of all the earth; but the Greek gods were limited to certain localities, and their power was indeed small. They were not the masters of men, but the allies of those who sacrificed upon their particu-

lar altars. If men did not feed them, they starved. The
Hebrew God was a god of blood, of vengeance, and jeal-
ousy; no one would venture to describe him or conceive
his appearance; he was infinite, immutable, omnipotent,
omniscient, absolutely independent both of necessity and
all external things; he ruled the whole universe by mere
fiat; he was passionless—in no way related to mortals.
But the Greek gods were beautiful and athletic men and
women, whose statues adorned the pagan cities; they
were full of all human passions and weaknesses; even
Zeus was as much subject to Fate as were mortal men.
The two races breathed their ideals into their deities.
The Levites were a powerful and domineering class;
among the Greeks, as wherever the one-world philosophy dominates, the representatives of religion were a
rather small, mediocre, and insignificant group,[8] which
did not constitute a class at all.

All the religion which the enlightened Greeks possessed may be said to have disappeared by the fourth century B.C. Certainly, by that time advanced minds considered the stories of Chronos, Saturn, and Jove myths
just as much as we do. Nevertheless, among the ignorant, the old tales were still accepted; and Socrates was
made to drink the hemlock because he had corrupted the
youth by bringing in new gods. Aristotle, Democritus,
Plato, Empedocles, and Xenophanes did not escape religious persecution; yet the intensity of religious feeling

[8] Note the treatment of Chryses by Agamemnon in Book I of the
Iliad. Yet Chryses was a priest of the sun-god Apollo.

among the Greeks was incomparably weak when balanced against that of the sixteenth and seventeenth centuries of Europe.

In metaphysics, the Greek philosophers were mon-
ists. This was very important. They thought all existence a manifestation of God—of one identical and underlying substance; and many, like Xenophanes—who
went the length of pantheism—declared this substance
to be God. Aristotle believed in a transcendent theism;
but there was no hint of metaphysical duality in his system. The point is that Greek thought considered the
Deity something very closely related to man and nature
at large; and all material things were deemed not only
real[9] and eternal but also good. As Nietzsche has pointed out, [10] the Greeks knew of *bad* things, but not of *evil*
ones. They saw nothing malicious in the world or in human nature; Homer praises the Trojans as much as the
Greeks and condemns Thersites, not because he is evil,
but because he is ridiculous.[11] Man, being a part of God

[9] The medievals, of course, looked upon this world as transient and
the city of the devil. That is partially the thesis of Augustine's *De Civitate Dei*. Plato, we see, does not belong with the other Greek philosophers in his metaphysical theory.

[10] *Genealogy of Morals*. The point is that Greek ethics are those of
a dominant race or caste; while Christian ethics are slave-morality, full
of vindictiveness and recrimination—the weapons of the weak and
downtrodden.

[11] As a contrast to this, we may consider the writings of the controversialists and party historians in Europe during the fourteenth to
the eighteenth centuries. Oldham's *Satires* upon the Jesuits are merely
typical of what was done everywhere. All reviled their opponents most

or at least closely related to him, was all excellent: no
part or attribute of him could be intrinsically bad; and
Greek statuary exhibits the human form in all its naked
majesty and beauty. The conviction of Augustine that
sex and sexual impulses are reprehensible would have
been totally unintelligible to the Greek.[12] Nor would
Paul's dualism between flesh and spirit have seemed less
incomprehensible.[13]

Hellenic ethics were exceedingly rationalistic. From
Socrates to Seneca the doctrine was taught that happiness is attainable only through human knowledge, and
wisdom. The Greek thinkers with one accord declared
that evil, misery, and ignorance are synonymous. Whatever religion their philosophers held was one of reason.
It is obvious that such a system throws great responsibility upon the individual, but, by way of compensation,
also confers large privileges upon him. It creates him the
judge of right and wrong; it makes the human intellect
the source of knowledge; it charges human degradation
and suffering and it credits human excellence and elevation to the account of man himself. It demands self-reli-

---

virulently. As an example of what schoolboys wrote, cf. Milton's "In
Quintum Novembris." The Devil was regularly represented as the direct ally of the pope, and effigies of the pair burned in London as late
as the eighteenth century. Such a phenomenon, of course, would have
been impossible among the Greeks.

[12] Cf. *De Civitate Dei*, Book XIV, chap. xvii–xxvii.

[13] Cf. Rom. 7:14–25.

ance and inculcates self-assertiveness. It constitutes man a self-directive and self-dependent unit.[14]

It is therefore not strange that the Greeks should have been lovers of freedom. This propensity found expression in many ways. All Hellenic philosophers maintained the ethical freedom of the will.[15] They demanded freedom of thought and expression. Socrates questioned and doubted all that was considered established: he was a skeptic, one who demanded untrammeled intellectual liberty. The Greeks lived much in the open air and rebelled at any kind of tyranny.[16] They reveled in the physical strength and intellectual energy which belong to a dominant race. The Greeks and the Romans were not merely free: there were the masters of all they surveyed. Nor were they subject to any crushing superstition.

Furthermore, they loved knowledge and activity. Knowledge, declared Socrates, Plato, Aristotle, and the Sophists, is the *summum bonum* of life. The Greeks' love for athletic contests symbolizes their love for action; they were intensely interested in what was about them. They made war; built cities; extended their conquests and commercial relations; carried on investigations in philosophy, mathematics, and science; educated their youth; and discussed public questions—all this they did with fervent activity. Athens, especially during

[14] For an excellent résumé of the whole development, cf. Windelband, *History of Philosophy*, pp. 72–87, 159–209.

[15] Cf. particularly Aristotle's *Ethics* and Seneca's *Morals*.

[16] Witness how they rose against the Persians.

the fifth century B.C., was a seething center of life, the business of which was to conquer in all realms—the material, the intellectual, and the artistic. Such a phenomenon, of course, would be utterly impossible under the Augustinian philosophy.

The Greeks loved activity and knowledge very much, but they loved beauty and art even more. At the Olympic games, poets and dramatists competed publicly for the laurel crown. The works of Aeschylus, Sophocles, Euripides, Homer, and Hesiod were the delight of the nation. Greek statuary, poetry, drama, philosophy, oratory, and architecture are unsurpassed, have been the wonder and despair of succeeding generations, and are still artistic models. In criticism, science, geometry, astronomy, and history they made contributions by no means contemptible.[17] In empirical science they had indeed made little progress; they did not apply the principles of the Baconian philosophy on any large scale, although Aristotle formulated the rule of inductive reasoning. Wherever great quantities of natural data are unnecessary, however, their generalizations and conclusions are as good as any that have since been made. Fer-

[17] Here a single word of caution is necessary. It is true that our age has far more in common with Periclean than with medieval life: yet we must not make the mistake of thinking that we have not developed far beyond the Greeks in certain respects. The ancient philosophers indeed made many shrewd guesses, which have been verified more or less exactly by modern science; but none of the great inventions which make modern life what it is were known to them. Yet their science and philosophy were such as could produce, when studied by men already interested in life and action, the great pagan Renaissance.

vent love of beauty and activity, worship of the superb
human form, and striving for perfection are qualities peculiarly Greek and classical and could never exist under
the Augustinian system.

The second great force in European history we call
"medievalism." This complex philosophy, which still exercises its influence in various places with varying degrees of intensity, was called into existence by several
causes, some general, others special, of which we shall
here mention only three of the former.

As the development of pagan ethical theory sufficiently proves, ancient life was growing more and more
corrupt with the passage of time. Overwhelming evidence indicates that by the time of Nero the population
as well as the court of Rome was inordinately depraved.
Rome was indeed a sink of iniquity. Every sin, every
profligacy, was common. But the penalty of sensual life
is a satiety and disgust which terminate in final despair,
and a loathing of life itself. Even the circus, the arena,
and unparalleled sexual immorality were incapable of
giving the jaded and debauched Romans a new thrill.
Man craved some remedy for the spiritual bankruptcy
attendant upon universal corruption.

Furthermore, history teaches that the Graeco-Ro-
man civilization had, by 100 A.D., nearly run its course.
It had expanded, become strong, developed artistically,
intellectually, politically, and scientifically: it reached
its peak in the Age of Pericles. But the sources of intellectual and creative energy soon ran dry; and, in the

transition from Greece to Rome, there was a uniform lowering in every department of life, except the political, military, and material. Poetry became imitative; criticism, as in Horace, came to consist of mere rules-of-thumb; philosophy descended from original metaphysics to imitative ethics. Rome exacted from tributary nations untold material wealth; but the Romans soon became enervated and effete; the heavy spear and shield fell from the arms of the legionaries. Man cannot live on bread alone; and when the intellectual and artistic genius of ancient paganism was spent, the whole fabric began to disintegrate.

The barbarian invasions were also a great historical factor. The weakness of the Roman Empire was indeed internal, but the pressure of the uncivilized tribes from the north made that impotence obvious. The rotten fabric might have stood much longer had it not been for the Vandals, the Suevi, the Goths, and the Huns. The whole length and breadth of the extensive empire was overrun and ravaged by these invaders; and in 410 A.D., Alaric sacked the Imperial City. It was just after this event, when all men's hopes were crushed, when the greatest empire the world had yet seen was crumbling, when the eyes of men saw nothing but scenes of woe and desolation, that Augustine wrote *The City of God*, to assure his fellow-Christians that, even though everything was failing here, Heaven is the certain reward of God's elect. What philosophy except one of surrender, defeat, and consolation could have prevailed during a time like that?

Every one who saw deeply into the existing evils perceived, even several centuries before the time of Augustine and Alaric, that some decisive remedy must be offered. And two great cures were propounded, in one great essential alike, but otherwise profoundly opposed. These were Christianity, completed by Augustine; and rationalistic ethics, consummated by Stoicism.

Christianity and Stoicism are alike in that they deny all real value to material things. Augustine assures his readers that, even though they have lost all their possessions, they have really forfeited nothing, for to the saints an eternity of heavenly joy remains.[18] The Christian considered this world worthless, not absolutely, but in comparison with the other. The Stoics felt contempt for material possessions and bodily comforts because of a somewhat different reason: they maintained that all happiness must consist in virtue, in well-doing, and that everything external to the mind is utterly indifferent to the good man—he who has subdued all his passions so that they are in the power of his will. And they condemned material things on moral grounds also. As long as we place our desires on such possessions, they said, it becomes our business to rob, to murder, to deceive. "If it is my interest to have an estate of land, it is my interest also to take it from my neighbor."[19] The Stoics sought to center man's attention on the excellence of the mind alone.

[18] Cf. *De Civitate Dei*, Book I, chap. ix.
[19] Epictetus, *Discourses*.

But apart from their attitude toward things worldly, the two systems differ widely. Augustinianism looks upon man as degraded in sin, a child of perdition, incapable of doing anything whatsoever for himself: he cannot, by his own power, even desire a good thing. If man is saved at all, he is redeemed by irresistible divine grace; he has no part in his own salvation. God picks a few at random from the mass of corruption, and saves them arbitrarily to show his transcendent mercy and power; for all men *deserve to perish*. This philosophy—the doctrine of externality—makes man distrustful of himself, convinced of his own worthlessness, unspeakably humble and abject. His chief business becomes the negation of his every natural impulse. With respect to the present state, this system is pessimistic even beyond the third and fourth books of *Gulliver's Travels*. The Stoic, on the other hand, is the exponent of the principle of internality: "Look within," said Marcus Aurelius; "within is the fountain of good." He sought to make man an impregnable rock of reasoning virtue which all the storms of passion, all the temptations of the world, must fail to disturb. The Christian looked forward to heaven; the Stoic believed that death is merely the cessation of sensation, a resolution of the individual, by which he loses his personal identity, back into the cosmos. Augustinianism requires faith, surrender, and self-abnegation, in return for which the individual receives endless bliss in heaven; in return for the contempt of all worldly things and the achievement of absolute self-dependence, Stoicism offers happiness in the consciousness of virtue—and nothing more. "Man is the measure of all things," and "Know thyself," said the Greek; "Throw yourself on the mercy of God," said the Christian, "for man is nothing." Augustinianism is comparatively easy, for it requires no strength to surrender; Stoicism is extraordinarily difficult. It is not strange, therefore, that one conquered Europe with amazing rapidity and that the other was left to be absorbed by only a few individuals like Pelagius, Erasmus, Milton, Emerson, Newman,[20] Thoreau, Schopenhauer, and Whitman.

The Aristotelian and the Christian virtues indicate the contrast between the pagan and the Augustinian ideals. According to the great Greek, the virtues are Justice, Courage, Temperance, Magnificence, Magnanimity, Liberality, Gentleness, Good Sense, and Wisdom. According to the Christian, they are Compassion, Good Works, Forgiveness, Love of your Enemies, Patience, Humility, Resignation, Surrender, Self-Abnegation, Faith, and Hope.

In order that our theological interpretation of Milton may be clear, it is necessary at this point to give a brief résumé of Christian doctrine. In this we will summarize the great dogmas called orthodox, and accepted almost *in toto* by the entire Roman Catholic Church and by all the Protestant reformers. There is very little di-

[20] Newman drew from Stoicism his theory concerning what education should do for a man. And, after all, are the moral and intellectual aspects really distinguishable?

vergence among theologians in regard to the great principles of Christianity; perhaps this fact is explained partly by their idolatry for what was old, accepted, and
authoritative; but much more by the fact that the system of Augustine was the most efficacious conceivable
for the purposes of a dogmatic church. And remember,
also, that we are not concerned with the origin of Christian doctrines: such problems as the historical existence
of Christ,[21] and the dependence of Christian beliefs upon
pagan myths[22] are beyond the scope of the present study.
The point is that for thirteen hundred years the dogmas
which we are about to outline were the most outstanding
and influential factor in European life; and it was against
them that Milton was in rebellion. It was the subversion
of these which brought the great Renaissance; which
made possible scientific activity; which freed man from
the most exacting and crushing intellectual slavery the
world has ever seen; and which, finally, resulted in the
"modernity" of the life we see about us. It is primarily
by virtue of his lifelong warfare against medieval philosophy and dogma that Milton may be called a man of the
modern world.

The fundamental assumption of early Christianity
was, as we have already intimated, that the present life
is worthless. This assumption resulted inevitably from
a great human experience. The dependencies of the Ro-

[21] Cf. J. M. Robertson's *Pagan Christs*. Many other works on the
subject have also appeared.

[22] Cf. Edward Carpenter's *Pagan and Christian Creeds;* Robertson's *Brief History of Christianity;* etc.

man Empire had been subjected to tyranny so long and
so thoroughly that surrender had become habitual to
them. It was but a short step from surrendering to an
earthly power to surrendering to a supernatural one. The
calamities visited upon the Jews were greater than those
of any other nation; and it is but natural that a religion
such as we are describing should have emanated largely
from them. And the experience of Rome itself, of which
we have already spoken, led to the same conviction
about the life of the senses. The ideal of early Christianity was escape from the world and its manifold misery. The early devotees gloried in speedy martyrdom,
and offered themselves eagerly to the Roman magistrates
as victims. If any fact is obvious in Christian literature,
it is that it pours contempt upon the world of sense.
Nay, it regards the life about us, not only as worthless,
but as immeasurably evil, to be avoided like a most dangerous disease. It is indeed difficult for us to realize this
attitude; but without doing so we cannot hope to understand the philosophy of Luther and Edwards—and of
the countless millions who have believed with them.

The first distinct conviction of early Christianity,
which provided the point of departure for its dogma, and
which it held in common with contemporary pagan
creeds long since forgotten, was the intense realization
of a belief in personal immortality. A man is born, they
said, into this world and lives here a period infinitely
short when compared with eternity. And at death begins
an endless existence in one of two places—in the fiery

torments of hell, or in the ecstatic raptures of the New Jerusalem. What shall I do to save my soul?—that was the burning issue, before which all other considerations faded into utter insignificance. In no other extensively prevalent philosophy do we find this intense realization of two eternal conditions, so utterly opposed and so vividly real, in the one or the other of which every human being must soon find his place.

The system would indeed have been an easy one to humanity had nothing but heaven, hell, and immortality been concerned in it. But such was not the case. Hell was to be avoided and heaven obtained by conditions neither few nor easy to meet. It was not that it would be difficult for the individual to deserve salvation, but that he was by nature excluded from it. It is easy to understand why the theologians should desire to make the terms as hard as possible, and why, therefore, many barriers, of which the scriptures contain scarcely a hint, should have been erected between the sinner and the Pearly Gates. Nevertheless, the Bible contains the germ of all Christian dogmas,[23] because doctrine was in its

[23] Of course, we must realize that dogma developed not chiefly out of the Bible, but out of human needs. Skilful controversialists have found equal basis in scripture for free-will and absolute predestination; for universal and specific grace; for the *creatio ex nihilo* and the mere re-formation of matter; for Trinitarianism and Unitarianism; and for hundreds of varying heresies. The authors of the Bible, of course, were totally unaware of the controversies which would later rage over its contents; and they express themselves clearly on no great metaphysical doctrine; nor have they a consistent point of view. The statement of the Catholic church that every man cannot satisfactorily formulate his own doctrines from scripture is surely well founded.

first stages of formulation when the various tracts, finally chosen to constitute the New Testament, were being composed.

The doctrine of human depravity is easily the most far-reaching of the Christian dogmas. This was certainly current before the Gospels were written, for we read there that the Father spared not his own, only-begotten Son, but sent him as a sacrifice for fallen man. Indeed, this was the central teaching of a half-score popular pagan religious sects which competed with Christianity and were marvelously similar to it. Humanity was lost in sin, hopelessly depraved, and, without vicarious atonement, could not hope for salvation. To deny this is to deny the validity of all historical Christianity. The doctrine is explained as follows by Augustine:

For God . . . . made man upright: who being willingly depraved and justly condemned, begot all his offspring under the same depravation and condemnation: for in him were we all. . . . . We had not our particular forms yet, but there was the seed of our natural propagation, which being corrupted by sin must needs produce man of that same nature, the slave to death, and the object of just condemnation: . . . . thence arose all this team of calamity, drawing all men on into misery (excepting God's saints) from their corrupted original, even to the beginning of the second death,[24] which has no end.[25]

This is the doctrine of original sin, according to which, as St. Bernard said, "Men are stinking spawn, sacks of dung, the food for worms."

[24] In theology, the second death was condemnation to everlasting torment.

[25] *De Civitate Dei*, XIII, 14.

To save man thus fallen, it was necessary that extraordinary machinery be erected. As every man was sunk in sin and could do nothing for himself, no mortal could be the savior: it was necessary that God give "his only begotten Son," to suffer and die for man's iniquity, to be the perfect sacrifice, to take upon himself the burden of the world's woe. The theory was that God would like to save all men; but, justice being his chief attribute, and man deserving the most terrible punishment, it was impossible, in the very nature of things, to save man without justification. Either man or justice would have to perish. Thus God himself became flesh and dwelt with us. It was necessary that he be God in order that he might elevate man to heaven; but it was necessary that he be man also in order that he might undergo and conquer every temptation to which we are subject. This was the mission of the Savior; and all who, like the Nestorians, questioned its supreme necessity were treated as most abominable and blasphemous heretics. This doctrine is most completely and philosophically explained by Anselm in his *Cur Deus Homo?* But every theologian repeated it. The great heresy of the Pelagians, the Socinians, and the modern Unitarians consists, of course, in denying the need of Christ's satisfaction. They make him a mere man, although an excellent exemplar; and they maintain that all men are able to save themselves through a life of virtue. They deprive the priest of his function.

A direct result of the preceding doctrine was one of

the great mysteries, the dogma of the Incarnation. It was necessary to explain how God could become man, and take upon himself flesh, without losing his godhead. Christ was born of a virgin,[26] of course without the agency of a human father. The Spirit of God overshadowed her, and she conceived a son, who "was of the substance of the Father, God of God, Light of Light, very God of very God . . . . being of one substance (ὁμοούσιος) with the Father and co-eternal with him.[27] But even this is rational when compared with the following: Christ consists of two separate and distinct natures, as is explained in detail in the creed of the Third Council of Constantinople, 680–81:

> Our Lord Jesus Christ must be confessed to be very God and very man . . . . consubstantial with the Father as touching his Godhead and consubstantial with us as touching his manhood; in all things like unto us, sin only excepted; . . . . one and the same Christ our Lord the only-begotten Son of two natures unconfusedly, unchangeably, inseparably, indivisibly to be recognized, the peculiarities of neither nature being lost by the union but rather the properties of each person being preserved concurring in one person . . . . defining all this, we likewise declare that in him are two natural wills, and two natural operations, indivisibly, unconvertibly, inseparably, inconfusedly, according to the teaching of the Holy Fathers.

In regard to the nature of Christ, there have been numerous heresies, of which the Arian is the most important. The Arians declared that Christ was not of the

[26] Like Mithra and many other pagan divinities.

[27] Creed of Nice, 325 A.D., *Nicene and Post-Nicene Fathers*, XIV, 3.

28   THE MODERNITY OF MILTON

same substance but of *like* substance (ὁμοιούσιος) with
the Father. The whole Catholic church split on this
question; and some of the most ferocious and devastat-
ing wars in European history were the result of the controversy. In the West, however, the more efficacious
though less rational doctrine prevailed, until it fell into
desuetude as a result of modern skepticism and indifference.

The Trinity, however, is the greatest metaphysical
doctrine of the church; Sir Thomas Browne calls it "that
wingy mystery in divinity." It consists of Father, Son,
and Holy Spirit, who are alike eternal, coequal, identical,
and consubstantial with each other—a tripersonal and
unified godhead. The members are distinct persons, with
differing functions, wills, and powers; yet they are "not
three gods, but one god,"[28] one in essence and constituting the same infinity. It was necessary, as we explained
in the foregoing, that Christ should be considered God;
but it would not do to make the Father the savior, as the
Patripassians did, for it was unthinkable that he should
suffer on the cross. There was mention also of a third
member, the Holy Spirit; and this, too, was elevated to
equality with the Father and the Son. Nothing else, perhaps, as incomprehensible as this has ever been accepted by a large number of educated men; yet many
enlightened people as late as the eighteenth century were
severely shocked to hear anyone question the validity of
this dogma. Servetus, even in the early part of the six-

[28] Athanasian Creed.

teenth century, it is true, called the orthodox Christians tri-theists; but he was burned by Calvin for his heresy. How three could be one and one three; how the Son could be consubstantial with the infinite Father who had begotten him; how both could be identical with the Spirit that proceeded from them conjointly—all this, and much more, was matter for implicit faith, and a stumbling block for countless heretics—to all, in fact, who reposed any confidence in human reason. The Trinity was, however, as Francis Cheynell declared, "the object of our faith"; it was the cornerstone of Christian theology.

But the goal and purpose of all the other dogmas is contained in the theory of redemption. This makes clear the means by which man may be saved, now that the satisfaction of Christ has been completed. The later Catholic church increased (for obvious reasons) the number of sacraments to seven; but all Christians have agreed that two—baptism and the holy communion—are essential to salvation. The latter of these especially has been the subject of endless controversy; the doctrine of consubstantiation, always held by the Catholic church, is that the bread and wine administered by the priest turns literally into the body and blood of Christ without apparent change. Without partaking of this communion, no man may, according to the doctrine of the Roman Catholic Church, hope to be saved. Largely by means of this eucharistic dogma—called that of the "Real Presence" —the Catholic church has been able to maintain an extraordinary hold upon its constituency, even in the twen-

tieth century. But the Reformers retreated from this
extreme position, and Zwingli went so far as to declare
the communion a mere symbolical rite, performed in
memory of the first holy supper administered by Christ
to his disciples.

In practical consequences, however, the dogma of
Absolute Predestination surpassed all others.[29] Without
going into detail, we may say that, according to this doctrine, God had, before the foundation of the world, determined whom of mankind he would make vessels of
wrath and whom he would make vessels of mercy. It
was necessary that God choose certain ones at random
out of the whole mass of corruption, for none were able
to do anything whatever for themselves; all were equally
bad—not able even to wish wisely. If God did nothing,
man was merely reprobated, that is, allowed to pass automatically into everlasting torment.[30] Reprobation was
the merest and strictest justice. If any man were made
one of the Elect, the action occurred as a result of God's
unmerited and infinite mercy.[31] According to Augustine,

[29] W. E. H. Lecky says that this belief has had more influence upon
mankind than any other speculative doctrine. Cf. *History of Rationalism*, I, 377.

[30] For a definition of reprobation, cf. Peter Martyr's *Common-
places* (London, 1583), III, 11*b*.

[31] In his *Anti-Arminianisme*, Prynne makes, under seven headings,
so fair and excellent a statement of the whole orthodox doctrine that I
will quote his words:

"1. That God from all eternity, hath by his immutable purpose
and Decree, predestinated unto life: not all men; not any indefinite or
undetermined, but only a certaine select number of particular men,

as we have already seen, man was created free, but became enslaved at the Fall; Calvin, however, took the ultimate step and declared that God decreed the Fall also. The theory of the enslaved will is the central doctrine of the Reformation; Arminius, who, very humbly and apologetically, denied its most repulsive and irrational im-

---

(commonly called the Elect . . . . :) which number can neither be augmented nor diminished: others hath hee eternally and perpetually reprobated unto death.

"2. That the onely moveing or efficient cause of Election, or Predestination unto life, is the meere good pleasure, love, free grace, and mercy of God; not the preconsideration of any foreseene faith, good workes, perseverance, good will, good endeavours, or any other prerequired quality or condition whatsoever in the persons elected.

"3. That . . . . the sole, the primarie cause of Reprobation or non-election . . . . is the meere free-will and pleasure of God: not the prevision, the pre-consideration of any actual sin, infidelity or finall impenitency in the persons rejected.

"4. That there is not any such Free-will, any such universal or sufficient grace communicated unto all men, whereby they may repent, beleeve, or be saved if they will themselves.

"5. That . . . . Christ Jesus died . . . . really, and effectually, for none but the Elect; for whom alone he hath actually impetrated, effectually obtained remission of sins, and life eternal.

"6. That the Elect doe alwaies obey, neither doe they, or can they finally or totally resist the inward powerfull, and effectuall call or working of Gods spirit in their hearts . . . . : neither is it in their own power, to convert, or not convert themselves, at that very instant time when they were converted.

"7. That true justifying, saving faith is proper and peculiar to the Elect alone, who . . . . though they sometimes fall . . . . into grievous sinnes . . . . never fall totally nor finally from the habits . . . . and state of Grace."

This incapacity for committing sin was called "the final perseverance of the saints."

plications, was perhaps the most hated and reviled[32] man in Europe during the seventeenth century. White-field and Edwards, armed with all the terrors of Calvinian theology, preached the depravity of man and absolute predestination during the eighteenth century; it was professed by many prominent preachers during the nineteenth, both in England and America. Now, however, like all Christian dogma, it is a curious relic of what was once omnipotent.

At the present time, we will glance at only one other doctrine—that of exclusive salvation. The theologians narrowed, as much as they could, the circle of those who might be saved. Before the advent of Christ, only a few special servants of God, who are mentioned in the Old Testament, were of the Elect, and those by the anticipated atonement of Christ. It was doubtful whether Solomon was redeemed, although Adam, the originator of sin, had been made a saint. All mankind, of course, except a few individuals, had gone to their place of torment. Furthermore, no one to whom the gospel of Christ had not been preached had any chance of salvation. But even among those who heard it, only those who accepted and believed implicitly could possibly have been selected as candidates for heaven. But no outward sign could prove saintship, nor was any obvious immorality disproof of it[33] in one whose creeds were correct. There

[32] King James I said that he wished that all Arminians might be put to death.

[33] Cf. the seventh point of Prynne's Creed, above, pp. 30 f. Cf. also Burns's humorous but correct poem, "Holy Willie's Prayer," which contains most pointed satire.

have been hundreds of sects; and each believed with fearful earnestness that those of its own exact persuasion would go to heaven and that all others would go to hell. Of course, the natural result of belief in exclusive salvation upon the individual was that he felt unutterably worthless in the sight of God; but it was no less an effect upon those who believed themselves elected that they became, under the guise of a humble spirit, immeasurably arrogant and intolerant toward all whom they considered reprobates. William Godwin was, during early life, strongly under the influence of Calvinism; he said that for a time he was fascinated by a teacher who, after Calvin had found a way of condemning 99 per cent of all Christians, had discovered a doctrine by which 99 per cent of even those could be sent to endless torture. The effects of this grim doctrine upon those who realized a belief in it, or who, being hypocrites, most inhumanly capitalized the power it gave them, were extraordinary and far-reaching. It gave rise to such mutual intolerance among Christians and such persecution against all whose opinions were unorthodox as are, without doubt, unequalled in human annals.

It is evident that these doctrines are supra-rational. They exist to establish the necessity of the church and of Christ's vicarious atonement and to save man hopelessly lost in his sins. The theologians did not reason mathematically, that is, inductively, from the known to the unknown, but legalistically, that is, deductively, from the unknown to the known. Bacon's great contribution was that he reversed the theological method of arriving at

conclusions and that he dealt, not with the metaphysical
and supernatural, but with the visible and the natural.
He helped to transfer the interest of thinking men from
the world of imagination to that of sense. None of the
doctrines of theology have any direct basis in experience,
nor are they comprehensible by reason. The Trinity, the
Incarnation, the *creatio ex nihilo,* are avowedly mysteries; and the theory of absolute predestination is ap-
parently unjust.[34] Luther, for example, made faith everything and action nothing in the process of salvation.
Thus, the whole system was frozen into irrational creeds,
from which the vitality had long since departed; and religion became something external, which its professor
comprehended little more than he understood the com-
position of the *primum mobile.*

The development which resulted in the doctrine of
absolute predestination and exclusive salvation is a very
interesting subject and may be traced in the works of
the Fathers. At the time of Justin Martyr (150 A.D.),
the Christian religion was still in an unsettled state; and
Justin, as he himself says,[35] was closely associated with
Stoics, Peripatetics, and Platonists. But progress was
rapid during the third century; and the Council of Nice
(325 A.D.) settled the great christological and trinitarian

[34] Calvin and Luther both admitted this, but said that it is our
impiety which makes it seem so to us. The position of Arminius, from
which he could not be routed, was this: if God decreed the Fall and
man had no choice but to commit sin, God is the author of evil: which
is impossible.

[35] Cf. his *Dialogue with Trypho.*

dogmas, against which heretics have ever since rebelled. It also determined by vote which books should be considered inspired and should constitute the New Testament. About 385, Jerome completed the Latin version of the Bible, which is called the *Vulgate*.

The Eastern church settled the theological problems dealing with Christ and the Trinity so thoroughly that these creeds lost their influence only by being forgotten; but it remained for the Western church to give a final solution to the anthropological problem, out of which the doctrine of absolute predestination was to develop.

Like Justin Martyr,[36] all the Eastern Fathers were deeply versed in, and much influenced by, pagan philosophers, especially Aristotle, Plato, and the Stoics. They are frequently invoked, and their ideas in regard to morality and free will were repeated in almost their exact words. Thus it happens that the oldest Fathers preached a Christianity quite different from that found in Western Europe. Like the Gospels of Matthew and Luke and the Epistle of James, they stress the worth of excellent action and maintain that man is rewarded for his virtue and condemned for his evil and that both are in his power: without qualification, man's will is free to do what it pleases. Such is the teaching of Clemens Al-

[36] He said, "And this is the nature of all that is made, to be capable of vice and virtue" (*Ante-Nicene Fathers*, I, 190); "Each man goes to everlasting punishment or salvation according to the value of his actions" (*ibid.*, p. 166).

exandrinus (153–217),[37] Athanasius (b. 300),[38] Gregory of Nyssa (b. 331), Basil (329–79),[39] and Cyril of Jerusalem (b. 315).[39] The teaching of the early Western Fathers was the same: Clement of Rome (*ca.* 100 A.D.),[39] and Lactantius (260–330)[39] (a favorite of Mil-

[37] Clemens is a child of Greek philosophy, to which he appeals at every turn; he praises human love, procreation, etc., in fact, much that later became anathema to the Roman Catholic Church, under the influence of ascetic philosophy. Many of his statements are literally copied from Aristotle and the Stoics. "This is the really good man, who is without passions . . . . having with virtue transcended the whole life of passion" (*Ante-Nicene Fathers*, II, 541). "Passions, then, are perturbations of the soul, contrary to nature, in disobedience to reason. But revolt and distraction and disobedience are in our own power, as obedience is in our power. Wherefore voluntary actions are judged" (*ibid.*, p. 361). "To be subjected, then, to the passions, and to yield to them is the extremest slavery; as to keep them in subjection is the only liberty" (*ibid.*, p. 378). "The Lord clearly shows sins and transgressions to be in our own power" (*ibid.*, p. 363).

That this is precisely the ethical theory of the Stoics is a matter easily determined. Cf. chap. ii *infra*.

[38] In the interests of Christ's godhead, Athanasius maintained the fallen nature of man; yet he asserted, in opposition to the oriental Gnostics, the Stoic doctrine of virtue, free will, and the internality of good. "Virtue hath need at our hands of willingness alone, since it is in us, and is formed from us. For when the soul hath its spiritual faculty in the natural state, virtue is formed. And it is in the natural state when it remains as it came into existence." It is indeed a far call from this to the doctrine of reprobation held by Augustine, Calvin, Luther, and the entire Western church. By the time of Athanasius, the Gnostics were becoming powerful; and he tries rather unintelligibly to combat their doctrine of evil. (Cf. *ibid.*, IV, 7.) He says, "The divine good is not something apart from our nature" (*ibid.* V, 358).

[39] These men repeat profusely the rationalistic Stoic and Peripatetic doctrines we have just been quoting. "Now men are wicked through ignorance of what is right and good" (Lactantius, *ibid.*, VII, 143).

ton)[40] were strenuous supporters of the doctrine of man's responsibility and inherent power of doing good or evil at his choice.

But another doctrine, destined to be triumphant, was already in evidence. It is obvious enough that the doctrine of absolute free will, which the Eastern Fathers preached, is fundamentally contradictory to that of human depravity, on which all theologians agreed. It is also evident that such an internal contradiction would soon prove subversive to all Christian dogma. It was essential that it should be made harmonious with itself, on this particular point; and such geniuses as Ambrose, Jerome, and, above all, Augustine, performed the momentous achievement.

Long before, Paul had taught, in a manner quite different from that of Luke, Matthew, or James, that the flesh overpowers the will and is intrinsically evil. Ambrose, the teacher of Augustine, declared himself dead in the sin of Adam.[41] And in Jerome (352–420), we find early hints of the doctrine of absolute predestination. He eschewed the pagan writers, he imagined himself scourged for reading Cicero,[42] and Paul was his oracle and inspiration. He says:

We never forget to thank the Giver: knowing that we are powerless unless he continually preserves us in His own gift. It is

[40] Cf. Milton, *P. W.* II, 386.

[41] *On the Death of Satyrus,* II, 6.

[42] Cf. *Nicene and Post-Nicene Fathers,* II, 35; and cf. Milton's ridiculing comment upon the passage, *P. W.* II, 64.

not enough for me, that he has given me grace once; He must give it to me always.[43] I am the hapless being against whom you ought to direct your insults, I who am for ever reading the words: "by grace ye are saved," and "blessed is he whose sin is covered." . . . . For while my spirit is strong and leads to life, my flesh is weak and draws me to death.[44] We know that the law is spiritual; but I am carnal, sold under sin. For that which I do, I know not; for what I would that I do not, but what I hate that I do.[45]

It is evident that the attitude of Athanasius cannot be one of absolute surrender, while that of Jerome must be one of utter humility.

But now we must say a few words about the work of Augustine.

The labors of this great theologian were chiefly expended in two great controversies: the Manichaean and the Pelagian.

Mani (b. 215) was a Persian who taught a universalizing religion, into which he tried to incorporate several distinctly Christian elements. His doctrine was one of absolute metaphysical dualism, which made no distinction between the physical and the ethical. There were, he said, two great uncreated and immutable forces in the universe, which he called by various names: one was God, the Light Principle, good, spirit, warmth, etc., —all of which are identical with each other; the other

[43] *Nicene and Post-Nicene Fathers*, VI, 278.

[44] *Ibid.*, p. 277.

[45] *Ibid.* Notice that this is nearly in the very words of Paul, Rom. 7:15; 19.

was the Devil, the Dark Principle, evil, matter, cold, etc., which are likewise but different names for the same thing. In the universe as a whole, in every portion of it, and in man, these opposite forces meet and remain in conflict. All material things, all physical impulses, and whatever gives pleasure to the senses are literally the Devil.[46] To attain excellence we must escape from and mortify the flesh—the body. This ascetic religion was absent among the Eastern Fathers, but it grew powerful in Rome about 375, so powerful, indeed, that it was a question whether Christianity or Manichaeism should survive. The two systems came to the death-grapple in the latter part of the fourth century and the beginning of the fifth.

One great element in Manichaeism caused Christianity to be its implacable foe. It made matter an original, uncreated principle, in itself immutably evil, itself a god as powerful as the god of light. The effect of this doctrine was to render the satisfaction of Christ null and void, the church unable to save fallen man. Manichaeism had to be stamped out, as a mortal enemy to Christianity. Augustine accomplished the task; and, in doing so, he propounded a doctrine of human nature and free will not opposed to that of Athanasius.[47]

But a greater struggle was at hand, in the course of

[46] This is the source of the old phrase "the world, the flesh, and the devil."

[47] It is because of the consequent change that Augustine may be quoted in support of both free will and predestination.

which the doctrine of redemption was given definitive expression.

About 409, Pelagius (a monk of Britain), who was under the same philosophic influence as Justin and Cyril had been, began to attract attention in Rome. He found that the state of morality was exceedingly low and that more attention was paid to creeds than to character. He and his bold disciples made a kind of Stoicism out of Christianity. They declared that Adam was created mortal; that his sin injured himself alone, having no affect upon posterity; that children are born without taint of sin and, if they die in infancy, go to heaven; that the law as well as the Gospel leads to salvation; that there were sinless men before the coming of Christ; that men can, by labor, make themselves perfect in the sight of God; and, finally, that every man's eternal fate is in his own hands. It is evident that this doctrine dispenses with the need both of the church and of Christ's vicarious atonement; and that, according to this, man needs no external machinery, no aid from outside himself, to achieve his salvation. Pelagianism is not Christianity at all; it immediately steps outside the limits of Christian philosophy.[48]

From 410 to his death in 430, Augustine exerted to the utmost his great intellectual powers to extirpate this

[48] The Socinians of the Reformation and the modern Unitarians are the religious descendants of the Pelagians. All deny human depravity, the divinity of Christ, and the personality of the Holy Spirit.

heresy,[49] which struck at the very heart of his religion. Augustine wrote from the depths of his own soul and from the bitterness of his own experiences. He everywhere emphasized the worthlessness, corruption, and degradation of man; he declared that, when Adam sinned, he plunged all his posterity irrevocably into the gulf of death, unless God, by his infinite power, draw him upward. Thus, fallen man becomes absolutely evil; but, as he was "created out of nothing," he is mutable and it is possible for God to transform his nature.[50] Consequently, as man is utterly incapable of doing anything for himself, even of wishing to be saved, salvation must be performed wholly by machinery over which he has no control. It is not difficult to see the trend of such a doctrine. The result was the dogma of absolute predes-

[49] In 418 and 419 laws of banishment and confiscation were passed against the Pelagians.

[50] We see here that Augustine had absorbed all but the consistency of the Manichee philosophy. He retains its essential dualism, but denies that matter is eternal. Here is the origin of the famous formula "created out of nothing," which the theologians devised in order to utilize the doctrine of Manichaean human degradation even while escaping its extreme implications in regard to matter as an evil, eternal, and immutable principle equal to God in potency. Mani declared the world, and consequently man, to be composed of this evil substance. But Augustine avoided Mani's conclusion—that Christ could not save man—by declaring that God created the world out of nothing.

Manichaeism had to be stamped out because it made salvation through Christ impossible; and Pelagianism had to be defeated because it made that salvation unnecessary. Augustine sailed the ship of Christian theology over stormy and treacherous seas; but he conducted it safely to port by avoiding both the Scylla of Mani and the Charybdis of Pelagius and by appropriating inconsistently whatever he could use.

tination, which has had, as implied above, larger consequences in the history of Europe than any other speculative conviction. It is certain that it was central in, and the very soul of, the Reformation; the influence of Augustine has been almost unrivalled in the Western church. Luther, Calvin, Knox, and Edwards were his implicit disciples.

Although Augustine denied the Manichaean doctrine maintaining the eternity and the immutability of matter, the metaphysical dualism which is its inevitable consequence is everywhere evident in the works of his maturity. The result was an unparalleled asceticism. Great numbers of men and women became celibates—thus denying the primal carnal instinct; they retired to monasteries and nunneries, hoping to deserve a better world by deserting this one. By mortifying the flesh, they hoped to conquer the world and the Devil. Hermits abstained from combing their hair, trimming their nails, or washing their persons. They slept on gridirons, dressed in hair shirts, and castigated their bodies.[51] Some of the more illustrious eremites lived constantly for many years on the top of monuments, exposed to all the elements,[52] until their flesh literally dropped from their bones because of its rottenness. Every form of art or amusement, of course, was fearfully condemned: for

[51] Even James II of England and Philip IV of Spain made a practice of this. Cf. Macaulay, *History of England.*

[52] Cf. particularly the life of St. Simeon Stylites in any encyclopedia or church history; or see Tennyson's poem about this famous ascetic.

these pandered to the indwelling Devil. Learning, being only a form of idolatry, fell into decay; Christian priests destroyed the remains of Greek culture with acrimonious fervency. For a thousand years only very few could read or write even a barbarous Latin. Little building was done, and no worldly projects were contemplated: men sought to gain salvation by a passive retreat from the world.[53] For the evils of the present, men compensated themselves amply by means of anticipated blessings. During the Christian Renaissance in England, the Puritans closed the theaters; whipped the players; prohibited dancing, flute-playing, and festivals about the Maypole; decreed Christmas a day of fasting and prayer; talked in a nasal twang; and were careful never to smile. They were suspicious of any poetry except that which combined the extremest barbarousness with the highest piety: for the honied sweetness of smooth verse must be a snare of the Devil. Francis Meres said (*Of Poetry and Poets,* 1598), "As the Anabaptists abhorre the liberal arts and sciences: so puritans and precisians detest poetrie and poems." The *Bay Psalm Book* illustrates how much sweetness the Puritans could tolerate.

Several other practical consequences of this philosophy were distinct and almost universal. Priests obtained vast wealth and usurped the political power: every one,

[53] The first really great acts of medievalism were the crusades, performed in the interests of the two-world theory of life. Nevertheless, the mere action which these required proves—like Christian, Renaissance art—that the philosophy which inspired them was beginning to break down.

good or bad, great or small, rich or poor, paid tribute to them. The pope became a great temporal prince, using his spiritual power to compel political enemies. By means of its seven sacraments, the church invaded every aspect of human existence. Without its consent and aid, the ordinary acts of human life could not be performed—neither burial nor marriage could take place.[54] A papal interdict was a more dreadful calamity than a pestilence, a famine, or a destructive war. Henry VIII set up to be an ecclesiastical as much as a regal prince. A history of the Middle Ages is largely a history of the Catholic church.

In the next place, Augustinianism reduces the individual to a political and religious nullity, because it credits him with no power of any kind that is his own, unless it be the power to do evil.[55] He must not presume to originate anything: for he is a mere puppet. Anselm's ontological proof of God's existence illustrates this: every man has an *idea* of God; if God had not put this into his mind, it could not be there; and therefore God exists. Had Anselm been told that man might create this idea for himself, the statement would, to him, have been absurd. Medieval Realism (the doctrine that man is a

[54] Under the interdict in England during the reign of King John, corpses were left unburied in the fields.

[55] This doctrine was so omnipresent that it is to be found clearly expressed even in the *Faerie Queene,* in spite of its fundamentally Hellenic and Renaissance spirit:

"If any strength we have, it is to ill,
But all the good is Gods, both power and eke the will."

mere shadow and has no actual existence) is Platonism bent to support the medieval doctrine concerning the individual. The divine right of kings may be considered a political result of this theory. The general consequence of all this, of course, was that man had to receive everything upon authority which he was told was the word of God. If anything thus told him seemed wrong, this only proved that he was incapable of comprehending the divine wisdom or that he was himself depraved and blinded by sin. By such means, it was possible to force upon men the most extraordinarily irrational and self-contradictory dogmas.[56]

The most obvious and universal characteristic of medieval thinking was its implicit belief in constant supernatural intervention. The medieval Christians derived their faith in miracles from the vulgar pagans; but the enlightened Greeks scoffed at them as much as does the modern skeptic. During the Middle Ages everything was explained in terms of the miraculous; no one understood the laws of nature, and so thousands of natural effects were attributed to the agency of angels or demons. It never occurred to people that results might be due to natural causes. That the monks made fortunes and rolled in wealth as a result of the ignorance and credulity of the frightened and unthinking multitude is a fact we all know. The blood of Thomas à Becket, which never ceased to flow from a fountain, proved a stream of

[56] One example of such contradiction was the doctrine of absolute predestination taught along with that of "good works."

gold to the priests of Canterbury. The ignorant popular imagination—under the control of priestcraft—peopled the skies and the woods with devils and other supernatural apparitions. Such late works as Increase Mather's *Remarkable Providences* and his son's *Wonders of the Invisible World* are monuments to the powerful hold which medieval superstition and ignorance had upon the human mind. Not even yet has the spread of knowledge been able to eradicate entirely this curse of the unthinking mind. But it is a remarkable fact that Milton, at a time when every one around him believed in miracles, never wrote a word indicating that he had any belief whatever in any miraculous occurrence.

A further result was that the tyranny, ignorance, and superstition of medieval life fostered an almost inconceivable corruption; the church as well as life in general soon became debased. That any man should be a liar, a thief, or a hypocrite is bad enough; but that one who has dedicated himself to the most holy of offices, professing to be the representative of God, should be all three seems monstrous indeed. Yet such, we know, was frequently the case. A pagan writer recorded that as soon as Christianity became the official religion, the men who had before pleaded for toleration fought for bishoprics like wild boars for a carcass. It was inevitable that self-seeking men should soon fill an institution which offered great temporal riches and power, without requiring much either of labor or of merit. Religion became less and less a life and more and more a ceremony and a spectacle. Morality and creeds were separated. Men needed but give obedience to the ecclesiastic, and verbal assent to his doctrines, and they could *do* as they chose. The business of the priest became to increase the power of his institution; and this could best be done by allowing all men to repay its services with money and recognition of absolute authority, and by leaving their conduct to their discretion. Thus Purgatory was invented, indulgences were sold, and dispensations given; monks received money for praying, etc.; numerous such profitable expedients were devised. Religion became a vast system of forms, which were in no way related either to conduct or to conviction; it appealed to the eye and the imagination and not to the mind or the reason. Chaucer, the author of *Piers Plowman,* Wycliffe, Erasmus, and Luther are only a few of a host of witnesses who have given us unexceptional evidence concerning the corruption of the late medieval church. Undoubtedly, there were still many sincere Christians; but, in general, religion was only dogma and show; religious conviction was nearly extinct by 1500.

Another great consequence of medieval dogma was a standard of values which would have been wholly abhorrent to the Greeks, and which seems revolting enough to us. A man was judged, not by his actions, not by his character, but by his opinions, his creeds. The great criminal was not—as under modern ethical standards— he who murdered, robbed, and burned, but he who questioned the authority of a priest or the truth of a dogma.

The greatest possible crime was to question the doctrine of the Trinity,[57] or to sell one's self to the Devil, as incredible numbers of "witches" were accused of having done. There have been hundreds of sects, who have all differed from the orthodox church upon some speculative point or other, such as child-baptism, predestination, or the humanity of Christ; and tens of thousands were ready to die and millions ready to burn others at the stake for their opinions. It is now impossible to realize or to overestimate the potency of these theological doctrines; an importance was attached to them far transcending anything else in human existence.

The last great result of the Augustinian philosophy was very widespread persecution and many horrible wars.[58] Death itself is indeed no great evil; but to live in constant fear of it is terrible. In Europe alone several

[57] Like the Arians, etc., among the ancients; and like Abailard, Servetus, and the Socinians among the modern heretics.

The reason that a heresy was such a great crime was, of course, that Christian dogma was considered the important thing in life. The present generation considers human life and property of paramount value, and therefore we punish crimes against these most severely. As soon as the interest in medieval Christianity (or the two-world theory of life) ceased to be powerful, its dogma became a matter of indifference, and persecution ceased because there was no longer zeal sufficient to maintain it. Notice how, in his *Letters from an American Farmer*, J. H. St. John de Crèvecoeur exults in the decrease in religious interest and the consequent tolerance and amity among the colonists.

[58] Witness the Thirty Years' War in Germany, and the wars of Justinian's reign; in these alone at least fifty millions perished. Remember also the Crusades, the wars in Ireland, in Holland, and the extirpation of the Albigenses. Contrast this with Greek and Roman antiquity.

millions have been put to death by ecclesiastical authority and judgment. Until about 1700, poor and helpless women were executed as witches; and the masses of people who watched them burn exhibited not the slightest compassion for the victims. In Spain the frequent *auto de fés*, at which, sometimes, hundreds were burned at once, were regarded as most pious and most acceptable offerings to a God whose chief attribute was justice. Calvin exulted in the murder of Servetus; and Luther was capable of advising that a "possessed" child should be thrown into a river to be cured or killed. Catholics and Protestants, as well as sects of both persuasions, persecuted each other with frenzied zeal. The authorities put down every vestige of heterodoxy or disobedience with unflinching perseverance and thoroughness. The Inquisition was called into existence by the Catholic church in the thirteenth century, and the *Index Expurgatorius* in the sixteenth, to extirpate heresy and rationalism. But the Protestants were no less rigorous, for, depending upon revelation and assuming infallibility in interpretation,[59] they persecuted with terrible zeal and for the glory of God. All the evils of modern life com-

[59] The following quotation is taken from Nathaniel Ward's *Simple Cobbler* (1647), and indicates accurately the universal intolerance of Milton's contemporaries: "It is said that men ought to have liberty of their conscience, and that it is persecution to debar them of it: I can rather stand amazed than reply to this: it is an astonishment to think that the brains of men should be parboiled in such ignorance. Let all the wits under the heavens lay their heads together and find an assertion worse than this . . . . I will petition to be chosen the universal idiot of the world."

bined weigh little when balanced against those of medieval and Reformation persecution. The cause of it,
which was the belief in exclusive salvation, is admirably
discussed by W. E. H. Lecky:

> If men believe with an intense and realizing faith that their
> own view of a disputed question is true beyond all possibility of
> mistake, if they further believe that those who adopt other views
> will be damned by the Almighty to an eternity of misery which,
> with the same moral disposition but with a different belief, they
> would have escaped, these men, sooner or later, will persecute to
> the full extent of their power.[60]

> Men were told that the Almighty, by the fiat of his uncon-
> trolled power, had called into being countless millions whom He
> knew to be destined to eternal, excruciating, unspeakable agony;
> that He had placed millions in such a position that such agony
> was inevitable; that He had prepared their place of torment and
> had kindled its undying flame; and that, prolonging their lives for-
> ever, in order that they might be forever wretched, He would make
> the contemplation of those sufferings an essential element of the
> happiness of the redeemed.[61]

How infinitesimal are the sufferings that man can inflict
upon man in comparison with an eternity in hell! Is it
strange, then, that under the Augustinian theology, the
saints grew calloused to human suffering and could ob-

[60] *History of Rationalism*, II, 11–12.

[61] *Ibid.*, p. 323. J. J. Rousseau also made it clear that the doctrine
of exclusive salvation was the cause of religious persecution. The following stanza from Wigglesworth's "Day of Judgment" indicates the
Puritan belief:

> "They live to lie in misery
> And bear eternal woe;
> And live they must whilst God is just,
> That he may plague them so."

serve the sizzling, writhing bodies of wretched burning heretics with complacent equanimity? There was a certain ineffable pleasure in torturing the minions of Satan and in giving them a slight foretaste of what would be their eternal condition. And if the redeemed in Paradise could enjoy such a spectacle, why should not they?

As a great spiritual force, the church had long been nugatory when the Renaissance swept over Europe from the fourteenth to the sixteenth centuries. Slowly but surely an interest in the present world and skepticism in regard to dogma had been growing up together. The worldliness of the church was condemned on all hands. The fact is that by the twelfth century Augustinianism was obsolete, because the conditions which had first called it into being existed no longer. Men began to feel that this world *was* worth while, and a Roger Bacon could construct a system of natural philosophy. The Christians learned much from the Mohammedans, whom they had regarded as barbarous infidels. The lower classes began to demand more rights;[62] inventions were made; and explorations were conducted. Rationalism sprang up in the universities and made progress among thinking men everywhere. And at the same time scholars turned to the great documents of pagan antiquity for inspiration and material. "The spirit of ancient Greece had arisen from the tomb and the fabric of superstition crumbled and tottered at her touch."[63]

The pagan Renaissance was a period of extraordi-

[62] Consider the peasant revolts both in England and in Germany.
[63] Lecky, *ibid.*, p. 251.

nary activity; it reveled in worldly achievement and sensuous beauty. It was a tremendous reaction against Augustinianism; all the energies and impulses natural to
man, which had been repressed and kept dormant for a
thousand years, were suddenly released. It was a time
of spontaneous and exuberant expression. Renaissance
art is unsurpassed in modern life. Its great cathedrals,
its painting, and some of its great poetry are inspired by
Christianity; but even these are pagan because they
bring the purely conceptual and spiritual into the sensuous and material. And most of its poetry and nearly all
its drama are overwhelmingly pagan in conception and
execution. Such a play as *Hamlet* or *Macbeth* and such
a poem as *Venus and Adonis* or the first two sestiads of
Hero and Leander are as far from the Christian attitude
as is *The Iliad, Oedipus Rex,* or a Pindaric ode.

But even as the Renaissance was a rebirth of pagan
interests and a reaction against Augustinianism, so the
Reformation, which did not delay long, was a rebirth of
the old Christian spirit and a reaction against the Renaissance. Medievalism was certainly not dead; in fact, it
is not extinct in the twentieth century. The Reformation
compelled the Roman Catholic Church to perform an internal reformation or go out of existence; it chose to reform, of course, and the Trentine Council was the effect
of the choice. The Catholics lost Scandinavia, Holland,
England, and half of Germany; but retained almost all
the rest. The intellectual, artistic, and physical activity
of the latter half of the sixteenth century in England was

equaled by the religious ferment and struggle of the second quarter of the seventeenth. It was in the midst of this religious furore that Milton's life occurred.

We should now be prepared to understand Milton's relation to Christianity. We may say that in his works up to 1655 there is no evidence that he had absorbed any essential portion of its philosophy. He had been immersed in controversy regarding political, ecclesiastical, and domestic problems; he had written about education, a free press, and English history. He had composed a number of poems of exquisite sweetness, filled with pagan imagery and morality. But he had done nothing to show that he was interested in religion for its own sake. The early Milton was a pagan, a child of Greece and the Renaissance. But after 1655 there was a marked change in his interests: he wrote *The Christian Doctrine, Paradise Lost, Paradise Regained, Samson Agonistes,* and, among others, a pamphlet explaining how hirelings might be removed from the church. He became a Christian. But his was not the religion of Bunyan or Prynne. At every turn we see the influence of rationalistic paganism in his Christianity. Everywhere it is more liberal and less dogmatic; it is more tolerant and rational; it is less narrow, and depends, never upon blind faith, but upon the consent of reason. Milton does not deny the need and efficacy of Christ's atonement; had he done so, he would have been a Pelagian—no Christian at all. But he denied the Trinity of personality; the dual nature of Christ; the doctrine of absolute predestination; the validity of child-baptism; the metaphysical dualism of Augustine; and the right of the civil magistrate to meddle with religion. He maintained that the Decalogue was abolished; that we must interpret scripture by individual reason; that the sacraments, being mere symbols, are not necessary to salvation; that body and spirit are one, inseparable, and equally good in essence; that not only divorce upon request but that polygamy is justifiable; that the church and state must be separated; that no man should receive pay for preaching; and other doctrines equally revolutionary—all subversive of medievalism and all tending to destroy the hold of dogma upon the human mind and to bring about the modern point of view. Wherever Milton exercised his great strength, he was a powerful force in disintegrating medievalism and all that it stands for, and in bringing about the modern era. He emphasized ethics, not dogma; his metaphysics[64] were such as to render Augustinianism null and void.

Religious development since Milton's time has more and more followed the line which he pursued. External pressure has caused the church to become more enlightened, and today we hear very little about original sin or hell-fire, which were once the chief themes for sermons. The Trinity, the Incarnation, absolute predestination, the need for implicit faith, the corruptness of fallen man, etc., are now little stressed. The Protestant

[64] He believed all substance identical with Deity and man essentially divine.

preachers deal chiefly with purely temporal problems, except where the congregations are very ignorant.

But this is not the principal result. The church has indeed undergone a remarkable evolution;[65] and general skepticism and higher criticism have exercised a comprehensive influence. But the significant fact is that the representatives of the Unseen have been shorn of the great powers which they possessed for so many centuries. Education, which they once controlled, has been secularized. During the last two centuries, statements, in literature of all kinds, implying the truth and necessity of belief in Christian dogmas have been gradually disappearing; and now they are not to be found, except in a few rather mediocre writings, which are avowedly religious. The light of reason, history, and philosophy has been brought to bear upon the origin and the nature of Christianity. The influence of the church is now largely limited to the persuasion exercised by her ministers in their pulpits; it has little civil or material power, and can no longer coerce those who do not care to accept its doctrines. Countless people of irreproachable character and high intelligence never enter a church, feeling that it has no message for them. And it exercises little terror over the minds of the bad and ignorant, who, during the Middle Ages, would have paid a high price for absolu-

[65] For example, for many centuries the church preached the extreme danger of depending upon morality for salvation; now it preaches little else than the need of morality. In 1870, the church preached the danger of science to religion; now it preaches their harmony. The science it could not combat successfully it now seeks to incorporate.

tion, because they never dreamed of questioning the doctrines of the church. Today thought is very free and tolerance comparatively liberal.[66] This is one result—although not perhaps the most significant—of such thought as Milton's. To what extent this consequence is good and to what extent it is evil, no one can perhaps say: but the reality of its influence is indubitable.

One great fact in our history at which we ought to rejoice is the disintegration of medievalism; no other progress could be made before this was well under way. The blessings of art, freedom, individuality, knowledge of human origins, scientific advancement, etc., which were thus made possible, are the greatest of which we know; mere material wealth and comfort weigh as nothing in the balance. We ought to pay a debt of gratitude to those champions of knowledge and of human right and reason who made modern life possible and who procured for us what we hold most dear. Of these champions, perhaps none is more important than John Milton, Englishman.[67]

[66] Thus it was that, during the last quarter of the nineteenth century, R. G. Ingersoll could, with his fluent and eloquent agnosticism, be a most popular lecturer, highly applauded by large and cultured audiences who paid a considerable price of admission to hear him. In 1927, Ingersoll, with the same message, would be uninteresting to similar audiences: new issues are before us.

[67] Sentimentalism, inspired by Rousseau, was the chief force in the eighteenth century disintegrative to Augustinianism. But the complete breakdown in English literature began with Hume, Gibbon, Godwin, and Paine; and was continued during the nineteenth century by such men as Shelley, Byron, Darwin, Swinburne, Meredith, Carpenter, Shaw, etc.

CHAPTER II

MILTON'S ETHICS: HIS RELATION TO PURITANISM AND STOICISM

Ethics may be defined as a theory of conduct or the science of human happiness. Ethics deal with social relationships or with a man's theory in regard to himself, and attempt to explain how he should act and why. A theory of ethics may depend largely upon metaphysics or theology but in itself is very different from these: metaphysics deal with what is beyond perception and experiment, what we imagine or suppose, not what we see or experience; theology, which is a branch of metaphysics, is literally the theory of God, and consists of doctrines the validity of which depends upon his constitution and his will. Such a theory is necessarily speculative. But a theory of ethics includes a man's conception of himself, is intensely practical, and determines not only his attitude toward himself and his fellow-men but also his actions in relation to them; it may even modify his belief concerning speculative problems, as was certainly the case with Milton.

We may distinguish between social ethics and individual ethics. The former is statutory law or the codified opinion of the majority, or the powerful, as to what is right and wrong, that is, what ought or ought not to be done; and this is enforceable by penalities of varying severity, ranging from a small fine to capital punishment. There is also a whole system of social ethics governing general human relationships which do not come under the penal laws, such as courtesy, aiding the distressed, etc. Lastly, all the rules of social etiquette may be said to belong to the realm of lighter social ethics. For the whole group, there is but a single theory, although this may vary widely during different historical periods, being always the systematized will of the majority or of the powerful. Heretics, non-conformists, individualists, criminals, are merely people who rebel against the general theory.

An individual system of ethics may be wholly different from the general and is always somewhat so. Although the mass of mankind are slaves to orthodox opinions, there are always independent minds capable of differing from the vulgar majority. But the important factor is this: public morality is a generalization, whereas personal ethics always depend upon the two following factors: first, what, in the opinion of the individual, is worth most in human life; second, his theory concerning his own powers and rights. Social and private ethics are both theories of conduct; but in the latter infinite variety necessarily exists simultaneously, all producing different individual attitudes toward life. It is evident that he who repudiates this world and takes refuge in another—as the bulk of humanity did in Europe during the Middle Ages—will have a theory of conduct widely different from that of the man who believes this to be an

excellent and the only world. Likewise, the Pelagian
and the Augustinian cannot have the same theory of ethics; nor can he who sacrifices the group to the individual
entertain the same doctrine of social relationships as
does he who sacrifices the individual to the group. The
rebel or the reformer is merely a man who tries systematically to make society accept his individual theory of conduct. Milton's ethical theory, then, must be
deeply significant in a philosophical interpretation of his
thought.

The objective of the present chapter is to show that
Milton's ethics are those of the Greeks in general and of
the Stoics in particular and that they are diametrically
opposed to the Puritan theory of conduct. It seems best
to develop this subject in the following manner: first, by
giving an exposition of Puritan ethics, in order that we
may realize the theory of conduct dominant in Milton's
day; second, by explaining, in some detail, Milton's own
theory, in order that we may know what he thought and
how he reacted toward those about him; and, third, by
giving a résumé of Greek and especially Stoic ethics, in
order that we may realize the source of his moral principles.

The first great element in Puritan ethics is its doctrine of anthropology—of which we have already spok-
en. With complete consonance, every orthodox theologian until the nineteenth century declared that man has
no power of being virtuous; that every natural action
must be evil; and that his nature—both physical and in-

tellectual—is corrupt and ruined, his very essence transformed into sinfulness. We cannot overestimate the dreadful strength and universality of this doctrine.[1] The only way to realize Puritan ethics is to read the statements of its authoritative representatives. As we have already seen, Athanasius maintained, in opposition to the Gnostics, both the inwardness of virtue and the freedom of the will. But he insisted no less on human depravity:

> Now if there were merely a misdemeanor in question and not a consequent corruption, repentence were well enough. But if when . . . . men became involved in that corruption which was their nature, and were deprived of the grace which they had . . . . what further step was needed?[2] [Therefore] the Word of God came in his own person.[3] Corruption in death was theirs [men's] by nature: no longer to live in Paradise, but . . . . to abide in death and destruction.[4]

But it was Augustine who made this doctrine the center of medieval Christianity and the basis for all its ethics. His teaching was accepted by all succeeding orthodox theologians until the nineteenth century. He de-

---

[1] John Cassian (360–448), who, because he revolted against Augustine's theory of absolute predestination, was considered heretical and is, technically, called a "semi-Pelagian," was quite orthodox on the question of man's fallen nature and the need of Christ's vicarious atonement; he wrote: "Their aim [the Pelagians' and Nestorians'] and endeavor was this: viz., that, by bringing Him [Christ] down to the level of common men, and making Him one of the common herd, they might assert that all men could, by their own life and deeds, secure whatever He had secured by his good life. A most dangerous and deadly assertion!" (*Nicene and Post-Nicene Fathers,* XI, 325.)

[2] *Ibid.,* IV, 40.   [3] *Ibid.,* p. 43.   [4] *Ibid.,* p. 38.

clared that Christ's atonement had no effect upon the mass of mankind, as Athanasius had believed. It merely enabled God, without being unjust, to save the few whom he had predestined to be the Elect. A few passages from various sources will serve to illustrate this doctrine of corruption and reprobation and its effects upon the minds of those who realized a belief in it.

Augustine explained his boyish desire to steal pears by the innate evil of his nature; he exclaims:

Nor cared I to enjoy what I stole, but joyed in the theft and sin itself. . . . . I loved to perish, I loved mine own fault. . . . . Foul soul, falling from Thy firmament to utter destruction![5]

When the genius of John Calvin gave utterance to the following, he stated the central position of Puritanism:

Let it stand as an indubitable truth, which no inquiries can shake, that the mind of man is so entirely alienated from the righteousness of God, that he cannot conceive, desire, or design anything but what is wicked, foul, impure, and iniquitous; that his heart is so thoroughly environed by sin, that it can breathe out nothing but corruption and rottenness.[6]

Bunyan's *Grace Abounding to the Chiefest of Sinners* is the story of how a man, convinced—beyond anything we can comprehend—of his own unspeakably great inherent evil, at last won salvation by supremely unmerited mercy. This book is a great human document and expresses the quintessence of English Puritanism. Bunyan thought his sins the most abominable enor-

[5] *Confessions.*   [6] *Institutes.*

mities in the world;[7] he spent days, and weeks, and months, and years in excruciating mental agony; he imagined that he had committed the unpardonable crime, that his breastbone was about to split, and that his bowels, like those of Judas, were about to burst. The Devil, he thought, was near him and within him constantly, prompting him to all manner of heinous transgression. Use your imagination, if you have a vivid one, to realize the extremely morbid psychological condition of him who wrote the following; and yet this condition was the essentially *normal* one among the Puritans. The following passages relate, first, how he committed the sin of Judas against the Holy Ghost; and, second, how the relief from his maddening apprehensions began:

But to be brief, one morning as I did lie in my bed, I was, as at other times, most fiercely assaulted with this temptation, *to sell, and part with Christ;* the wicked suggestion still running in my mind, *Sell him, sell him, sell him, sell him, sell him,* as fast as a man could speak: Against which also, in my mind, as at other times, I answered, *No, no, not for thousands, thousands, thousands,* at least twenty times together: But at last, after much striving, even until I was almost out of breath, I felt this thought pass through my heart, *Let him go, if he will;* and I thought also that I felt my heart freely consent thereto. Oh, the diligence of Satan! Oh, the desperateness of Man's heart!

Now was the battle won, and down fell I, as a Bird that is shot from the top of a tree, into great guilt, and fearful despair. Thus getting out of my bed, I went mopeing into the field; but, God knows, with as heavy an heart as mortal man, I think, could

[7] The worst of these seems to have been a desire to ring the bell in a church steeple.

bear; where for the space of two hours, I was like a man bereft of life, and as now past all recovery, and bound over to eternal punishment.

. . . .

Now was I as one bound, I felt my self shut up unto the Judgment to come; nothing now, for two years together, would abide with me, but damnation, and an expectation of damnation. . . . .

These words were to my soul, like fetters of Brass to my legs; in the continual sound of which, I went for several months together. But about ten or eleven a-clock on that day, as I was walking under an hedge (full of sorrow and guilt, God knows) and bemoaning my self for this hard hap, that such a thought should arise within me, suddainly this sentence bolted in on me, *The blood of Christ remits all guilt.* At this, I made a stand in my spirit: With that, this word took hold upon me, *The blood of Jesus Christ his Son, cleanseth us from all sin.* . . . .

. . . .

Once, as I was walking to and fro in a good man's shop, bemoaning of my self in my sad and doleful state, afflicting my self with self-abhorrence for this wicked and ungodly thought; lamenting also this hard hap of mine, for that I should commit so great a sin, greatly fearing I should not be pardoned; praying also in my heart, that if this sin of mine did differ from that against the Holy Ghost, the Lord would shew it me: and being now ready to sink with fear, suddainly there was as if there had rushed in at the window, the noise of wind upon me, but very pleasant, and as if I had heard a voice speaking, *Didst ever refuse to be justified by the Blood of Christ?* And withal, my whole life of profession past, was in a moment opened to me, wherein I was made to see, that designedly I had not: So my heart answered groaningly, *No.* Then fell with power that Word of God upon me, *See that you refuse not him that speaketh,* Heb. 12. 25. This made a strange seisure upon my spirit, it brought light with it, and commanded a silence in my heart of all those tumultuous thoughts that before

did use, like masterless hell-hounds, to roar and bellow, and make
an hideous noise within me. It shewed me also, that Jesus Christ
had yet a word of Grace and Mercy for me, that he had not, as I
had feared, quite forsaken and cast off my Soul.

In Edwards' *Personal Narrative*, we obtain a clear
view of that unutterable self-abnegation before God
which was the chief manifestation of Puritanism:

My wickedness, as I am in myself, has long appeared to me
perfectly ineffable, and swallowing up all thought and imagination;
like an infinite deluge, or mountains over my head. I know not
how to express better what my sins appear to me to be, than by
heaping infinite upon infinite, and multiplying infinite by infinite.
. . . . When I look into my heart, and take a view of my wickedness, it looks like an abyss infinitely deeper than hell. . . . . And
yet it seems to me, that my conviction of sin is exceedingly small,
and faint; it is enough to amaze me that I have no more sense of
my sin. . . . .

I have greatly longed of late for a broken heart, and to lie
low before God; . . . . it would be a vile self-exaltation in me,
not to be the lowest in humility of all mankind. . . . . And it is
affecting to think, how ignorant I was, when a young Christian, of
the bottomless, infinite, depths of wickedness, pride, hyprocisy,
and deceit left in my heart.

Nor are the statements of carefully worded and authoritative creeds at all different. They are unanimous
in condemning every heresy which gives man the slightest part in the work of his own salvation.[8]

[8] In the *Formula of Concord*, for example, occurs the following
statement: "We reject also the false dogma of the Semi-Pelagians who
teach that man by his own powers can commence his own conversion
but can not fully accomplish it, without the grace of the Holy Spirit."

Out of the Puritan doctrine of man's utter wickedness and depravity came that of his unqualified inability
to do anything of spiritual benefit for himself. This is
implied by the whole external system of machinery by
which man was to be saved; it is maintained in all the
Protestant creeds; and, in the following quotations, it is
stated both fairly and adequately:

There is an absolute and universal dependence of the redeemed upon God.[9]

The soul of a true Christian . . . . appeared . . . . low and
humble on the ground. . . . . My heart panted after this, to be
low before God, as in the dust; that I might be nothing, and that
God might be ALL.[10]

And again:

My experience [has since] . . . . taught me . . . . my extreme feebleness and impotence, every manner of way; and the
bottomless depths of secret corruption and deceit there was in my
heart.[10]

Luther made self-abnegating humility the central
doctrine of his creed, the source of justification:

The saints have their sins ever before them, they beg for
righteousness through the mercy of God and, for that very reason,
they are always accounted righteous by God; in truth, they are
sinners, though righteous by imputation; unconsciously righteous
and consciously unrighteous, sinners in deed but righteous in hope.
. . . . When we are convinced that we are unrighteous and without the fear of God, when, thus humbled, we acknowledge ourselves to be godless and foolish, then we deserve to be justified by

[9] Edwards, "God Glorified in Man's Dependence."

[10] Edwards, *Personal Narrative*.

Him. . . . . There is nothing so righteous that it is not unrighteous, nothing so true that it is not a lie, nothing so pure that it is
not filthy and profane before God.[11]

Obviously, this doctrine is calculated to induce unparalleled humility and to reduce self-assertiveness to a
minimum. Puritanism—in fact, all medieval Christianity—saw no worth in action; its ideal was faith and passive contemplation concerning one's sins. By motionless
adoration of the Deity, the votary was achieving an escape from his own flesh and the world, drawing nearer to
God, and becoming slowly engulfed in his spiritual abyss.
Any action performed by depraved man and determined
by his depraved will must be evil: that was the belief of
Augustine and Luther. The Puritans did not build cities,
extend commerce, mine the earth, or write *belles lettres*.
The consequences of their philosophy is made clear by
Edwards, who, having absorbed its attitude and systematized its thought as only a scholar and recluse can, was
able to give supremely accurate expression to both:

My mind was greatly fixed on divine things; almost perpetually in the contemplation of them. I spent most of my time in
thinking of divine things, year after year; often walking alone in
the woods and solitary places, for meditation, soliloquy, and
prayer, and converse with God.

Thus, it was natural that, to discover the truth, the
Puritan would appeal, never to man's depraved reason,
but to authority. Orthodox theologians appealed to their
predecessors, to the creeds, to the Fathers and, above all,

[11] H. Grisar, *Luther,* I, 218–19.

to the infallible revelation contained in the Bible; they
never appealed to man's sense of right and wrong, his
perception of truth or falsehood. Even Milton's *Christian Doctrine*, heretical as it was, is filled with biblical
quotations and references. He used the prevailing methods to destroy the prevailing dogmas; he supported rationalistic argument by theological methods; he met his
opponents on their own ground, proving their own authority contrary to their own doctrines. An excellent
example illustrating theological appeal to authority is
Prynne's *Anti-Arminianisme*,[12] in which he undertakes
to crush forever the new and invidious heresy, which he
declares as bad as Pelagianism. Prynne[13] had read widely in religious literature; he quoted so glibly and so extensively and made so many references that he was
called "marginal Prynne." His book against the Arminians is an appeal to authority par excellence: it is
nothing else. He quotes from all the English creeds; he
quotes from the writings of forty divines; and he says:

[12] London, 1630. Arminius (d. 1609) had merely maintained that
God did not decree Adam's fall and that God's predestination was general, not special, that is, that God simply determined the conditions of
salvation but left all men to observe or reject them.

[13] In a pamphlet of 1659, Milton speaks thus of Prynne: "A late
hot querist for tithes, whom ye may know by his wits lying ever beside
him in the margin to be ever beside his wits in the text, a fierce reformer once, now rankled by a contrary heat" (*P. W.*, III, 17). Prynne,
of course, is best known for his *Histriomastix: or a Scourge for Stage
Players*, 1633, which was a most bitter attack upon the theater as an institution and which was written from the typically Puritan point of
view.

If then all these give up their joynt and several suffrages for
our Anti-Arminian conclusions; if they all passe Sentence against
their opposite Arminian Errors (as this present Treatise will unde-
niably prove them to have done) you may confidently declare, re-
solve, re-establish the one as being; exile, yea, damne, the other as
not being, the Ancient, received and undoubted Doctrine of the
English church.[14]

He is not concerned with rational judgment; he merely
asserts that what has been accepted must be accepted
now; no individual may presume to originate a new doctrine, or to overturn an old one.

It is impossible that the human mind should be better prepared for the acceptance of irrational dogma than
by such a theory of ethics as we have just delineated.
And it is obvious that it was simply a repudiation of the
validity of human reason. The theologians gloried in the
fact that reason could not comprehend their teachings,
that human understanding was no factor in religion, and
that man must bow down before God in unquestioning
faith. Augustine said:

O man, who art thou? Faithful ignorance is better than pre-
sumptuous knowledge. Seek merits and you will find nothing but
punishment. . . . . Do you seek a reason? I will tremble at the
depth. Do you reason? I will wonder. Do you despise? I will believe. . . . . Paul . . . . calls the judgments of God unsearchable, and

[14] *Anti-Arminianisme*, "Epistle Dedicatory." In one very curious
passage seeking to render Arminianism ridiculous, he compares it to
Copernicus' theory of the universe, calling both monstrously absurd.
Prynne was perhaps both the most outstanding and most typical representative of Puritanism.

are you come to scrutinize them? He says, his ways are past finding out; and are you come to investigate them?[15]

Quotations of this nature could be made *ad infini-
tum,* but I will allow myself only one or two more.[16] Luther said:

This is the acme of faith, to believe that He is merciful who
saves so few and who condemns so many. . . . . If by any effort
of the reason I could conceive how God could be merciful and
just who shows so much anger and iniquity there would be no need
of faith.[17]

The ideal of mortifying the reason was almost as great
as that of mortifying the flesh—for both were equally
evil. Francis Cheynell—one of the framers of the *Westminster Confession*—exclaims vehemently and at length
against all who believe that human reason is at all capable of distinguishing truth:

Learn the first lesson of Christianity, Self-denial; deny your
will, and submit yourselves to Gods; deny your reason, and submit to Faith; . . . . Remember that master Chillingworth did
runne mad with reason, and so lost his reason and religion at once;
. . . . his reason was to be the judge, whether or no there be a
God? Whether or no that God wrote any Booke? . . . . What is

[15] Quoted in Calvin's *Institutes.*

[16] It is interesting to notice the contrast which J. H. Newman
makes between the methods of obtaining truth in theology and science.
He believes, of course, that human reason has no active—only a passive
—function in religion. And he wrote about 1850. Cf. *On University
Education,* "Everyman Series," p. 218.

[17] *De Servo Arbitrio.*

the sense of those books? What religion is best? . . . . Come, do
not wrangle, but believe your God.[18]

But the most curious and significant passage of this
kind of which I know is in Sir Thomas Browne's *Religio
Medici,* written about 1640. It is natural enough that
theologians should have gloried in the supra-rational
quality of Christianity; but that a skeptical physician
should have subscribed to it without reserve is a very
different matter. But clergy and laity, learned and vulgar, were all under the same powerful and omnipresent
influence.

Methinks there be not impossibilities enough in religion, for
an active faith; the deepest mysteries ours contains have not only
been illustrated, but maintained by syllogism, and the rule of reason: I love to lose myself in a mystery, to pursue my reason to an
O altitudo! 'Tis my solitary recreation to pose my apprehension

[18] *Rise, Growth, and Danger of Socinianisme* (London, 1643). We
must remember that Chillingworth's only crime—like that of Sir John
Davies about forty years earlier—was that he tried to prove the truth
of orthodox dogma, not by authority, but by reason. The following
passages from the book just quoted are most significant concerning the
problem we are discussing, and present a direct contrast to what Milton
was saying at the same time: "He [Socinus] taught the world a new
way of disputing in Divinity; we were wont to argue this: Whatsoever God said is true; [but the Socinians say] . . . . it is absurd to think
that God said anything but truth, and therefore unless it appeare by
some demonstrative argument that such a proposition is true . . . . we
must goe look out for some other sense which is agreeable to right reason." "The Socinian Errour is Fundamental, they deny Christ's satisfaction and so overthrow . . . . the foundation of our justification; they
deny the Holy Trinity and take away the Object of our Faith . . . .
they deny originall sinne and so take away the ground of our Humiliation, and indeed the necessity of regeneration; they advance the power
of Nature, and destroy the efficacy of Grace."

with those involved enigmas and riddles of the trinity, with incarnation and resurrection. I can answer all the objections of Satan and my rebellious reason, with that odd resolution I learned from Tertullian, *Certum est quia impossibile est.* I desire to exercise my faith in the difficultest point; for to credit ordinary and visible objects, is not faith, but persuasion.

Medieval and Reformation Christianity expressed itself in at least a score of great authoritative and essentially agreeing creeds. Seven Ecumenical Councils and the Council of Trent formulated the doctrine of the Catholic church. The Augsburg Confession, the Formula of Concord, the Thirty-Nine Articles, and the Westminster Confession are only four of many great Protestant creeds. All of these state simply and finally what every one, in order to be saved, must accept implicitly; if he wavers on any point, he is lost—devoted to an eternal and excruciating torture. The necessary result of such a system is that emphasis is placed upon faith and not on action; upon obedience, not upon self-assertion; upon professed creed, not upon morality. The Puritan, so far from praising civic virtue, looked upon it very suspiciously, fearing that it might seduce its owner to pride and self-reliance.[19] Luther said, "Away with all trust in righteousness; . . . . destroy all presumption in wholesome despair."[20]

The ideal of the Puritan was conformity to authori-

[19] Emerson's doctrine of self-reliance and Whitman's principle of egotism are, of course, diametrically opposed to all Puritan ethics. Cf. particularly the "Divinity School Address," an excellent analysis of historical Christianity from Emerson's point of view.

[20] Grisar, *Luther*, I, 218.

tative creeds and uniformity to given standards. Nothing could be more repugnant or abhorrent to him than any divergence on a point of speculative doctrine. His philosophy was a strait-jacket, into which every human being had to be fitted. Sectaries and heretics were his peculiar abomination. His system left no room whatever for individuality, for even the slightest difference of opinion, for any contribution of the self. One iron-clad rule was laid upon all, and its tyranny was absolute over man's reason. It is true that the Reformation transferred religious authority from a man[21] and an ecclesiastical tradition[22] to a Book and that, in theory, every man was to interpret this book for himself. But Calvin did not hesitate to do all in his power to cause a great thinker[23] to be burned at the stake, a thinker who professed to draw all his doctrines from the Bible alone, who stood ready to demonstrate the truth of his statement, but whose interpretation was not orthodox. The theologians assumed that they alone apprehended the sense of scripture; and they stood ready to persecute to the full extent of their power, or to kill, all who might question that assumption. Under such a system the proposition that men ought to be permitted to say what to them seems right must be intolerable. Puritanism saw in man a creature wholly destitute of intrinsic resources or human rights.

[21] The pope.
[22] The codified belief of the Holy Roman Church.
[23] Servetus.

To summarize, we may say that the Puritan was the exponent of the principle of externality, which was the basis of his ethics. I mean by this that for him nothing came from within man himself. He had no inward ethical strength. He made man but the shadow of will and reality. He was exceedingly humble and self-degrading before the powers of the unseen because he was burdened with the thought that he possessed no actual or even potential merit, that all good to him must be not the result of his own will and endeavor, even to the slightest degree, but a sheer and undeserved gift. Spiritually, he was a slave. Realizing his own impotence, he bowed down in absolute despair.

We are now prepared to see the contrast between the ethics of the Puritan and of Milton. Before going into detail concerning Milton's system, it may, however, be well to record a few external facts which indicate his opposition to the religion dominant in his day. His mind luxuriated in mythological allusion and in sensuous beauty, as we see in all his early poetry especially and as we learn by his own statement.[24] The Puritans regarded the

[24] He says in a letter to his friend Deodati, written in 1637: "Whatever the Deity may have bestowed upon me in other respects, he has certainly inspired me, if any ever were inspired, with a passion for the good and fair. Nor did Ceres, according to the fable, ever seek her daughter Proserpine with such unceasing solicitude, as I have sought . . . . this perfect model of the beautiful in all the forms and appearances of things. . . . . I am wont day and night to continue my search." Contrast this with Augustine's attitude toward the sensuously beautiful; cf. *Confessions*, "Everyman Series," pp. 64–65.

theater with vindictive malevolence; but Milton tells us in "L'Allegro" that he enjoyed Jonson's and Shakespeare's comedies, and, in "Il Penseroso," that he loved to see "gorgeous Tragedy, In sceptered pall, come sweeping by." When he thought, in 1641, that the Presbyterians were fighting for human liberty, he joined hands with them against the prelates of the Episcopal church. But when he found that one set of tyrants had merely been replaced by a worse, he declared that "New Presbyter is but Old Priest writ large."[25] After 1644, Milton was the implacable foe of the Presbyterians,[26] and he never lost an opportunity to taunt or deride them. In 1659, he wrote against tithes, which Prynne had just before defended. In the last year of his life, Milton published a tract asking equal toleration for Calvinists, Lutherans, Socinians, Arminians, etc. This, of course, was directly contrary to the principles of those who framed the Westminster Confession. But the most decisive external proof of Milton's opposition to the Presbyterians is contained in his *Christian Doctrine*. Here he denied almost every dogma proclaimed from their pulpits.[27]

It is true that Milton's ethics, like his thought in gen-

[25] This is confirmed by a passage containing exactly the same thought and using almost the same words in the *Areopagitica, P. W.,* II, 83.

[26] Who are to be considered practically identical with the Puritans.

[27] By virtue of an *Ordinance for the Suppression of Blasphemies and Heresies,* published by the Presbyterian parliament in 1648, Milton might have been charged with five capital crimes and eight involving indefinite imprisonment, had his *Christian Doctrine* been available then.

eral, underwent a distinct evolution. The unqualified independence and self-assertiveness of his early thought had been much modified when he composed *Paradise Lost* and the *Christian Doctrine*. Heaven was no longer the mere servant of man; nor was man any longer able to do everything for himself. Yet all the essential features of his early Hellenic ethics left a profound impression upon his mature Christianity.

For the sake of convenience, we may make a division in Milton's ethical system: first, those ideals which pertain directly to each individual; and second, those general and philosophical laws which apply to the life of an organized society. In the former class, we find the following principles: (1) that the individual is capable of being and should be a self-determining unit in matters of religious conviction; (2) that virtue, reason, freedom, and happiness are an indissoluble quaternity; (3) that the external should be sacrificed to the internal; (4) that self-discipline is of paramount value; and (5) that, if passion is allowed to rule over reason, the results will be disastrous. The fundamental philosophical principles which should govern all theory of social organization are, according to Milton, the following: rationalism, individualism, and the Principle of Internality. We will discuss these in order.

And we should notice that in every detail and principle of his ethics Milton was in direct revolt against Puritanism and in agreement with modern belief. Augustinianism allowed the individual no religious autono-

my; it denied that human virtue or reason could in any
way be related to freedom or happiness; it made all good
external to the individual; it repudiated the possibility
of active self-discipline; and it recognized no such faculty of reason in man as that which Milton made of paramount importance. As we have already pointed out,
nothing more irrational and unjust than medieval dogma
has ever been accepted by thinking men. Furthermore,
as we have also seen, dogmatic theology was a system
that utterly obliterated the individual in the scheme of
things, making of him a mere shadowy form. Finally,
and most important of all, Augustinianism was the principle of externality because it compelled man to receive
all good from without; Milton proclaimed that ethical
reality exists within the mind alone.

First, let us consider his personal ethics. The primary doctrine here is that the individual should be self-
determining in matters of belief. To be so is not only a
right but a duty and a necessity. He not only may, but
he must, work out for himself the principles he accepts.
Milton said:

> A man may be a heretic in the truth; and if he believe things
> only because his pastor says so, or the Assembly so determines,
> without knowing other reason, though his belief be true, yet the
> very truth he holds becomes his heresy.

This is far-reaching doctrine! Whatever truth a man
accepts without understanding it, is, for him, a falsehood. Yet the same theory is implicit everywhere in Milton's works—in *Comus*, in the pamphlets, and in *Paradise Lost*. Eve, for example, says: "We live, law to our-

selves." And we read in the *Areopagitica:* "God uses
not to captivate man under a perpetual childhood of pre-
scription, but trusts him with the gift of reason to be his
own chooser." "Things . . . . in religion, if not voluntary, become a sin." This, of course, is diametrically opposed to Puritan ideals.[28]

We find, next, that virtue, reason, freedom, and happiness constitute a moral tetrad. By obedience to reason,
man achieves virtue, which, in turn, confers freedom
upon him automatically; and the inevitable result is happiness. "Love virtue, she alone is free," the young poet
enthusiastically exhorts and proclaims. "If you think
slavery an intolerable evil," he says later, "learn obedience to reason and the government of yourselves." Before a man can be either virtuous or free, then, he must
be obedient to reason; this we learn from the following
also:

> But God left free the Will, for what obeyes
> Reason, is free, and Reason he made right.

Milton repeatedly declares that only the virtuous can be
free: "For, indeed, none can love freedom heartily, but
good men. The rest love not freedom, but license." He
declares,

Know, that to be free is the same thing as to be pious, to be
wise, to be temperate and just, to be frugal and abstinent, and,
lastly, to be magnanimous and brave; so to be the opposite of all
these is the same as to be a slave.

[28] Cheynell condemns the Socinians as the worst of all heretics because "They of all men do most affect the conduct of their own private
spirit, which they call Right Reason." Cf. above, note, p. 70.

Man possesses, we are told distinctly,

> Happiness in his power, left free to Will.

The *summum bonum* of life, then, is to be found in virtue and freedom, which result from obedience to reason and which issue in self-contained happiness.

It is evident throughout the works of Milton that he considers the internal of paramount importance. He agreed with the Puritans in considering material things of small worth, but for a very different reason. They hated this world because it was of the Devil; and this sweeping condemnation included all artistic and intellectual activities. Milton worshiped these latter; but he contemned material things because they are without ethical valuation and because the integrity of the mind is the sole great treasure. In a letter to his former tutor, Thomas Young, he wrote, in 1628, felicitating him upon his life on his little farm, where he lived

> with a moderate fortune, but a princely mind; and where you practice the contempt, and triumph over the temptations of ambition, pomp, luxury, and all that follows the chariot of fortune, or attracts the gaze and admiration of the thoughtless multitude.

And this sentiment, which we find often repeated in his works, he amply confirmed forty years later in *Paradise Regained:*

> Extoll not Riches then, the toyl of Fools,
> The wise mans cumbrance, if not snare;
>
> . . . .
>
> But to guide Nations in the way of truth
> . . . . . this attracts the soul,
> Governs the inner man, the nobler part. . . . .

It is obvious that while the rule of a political tyrant
seemed base to Milton, that of the philosopher seemed
most noble. He did not care to occupy a place in the sun;
he wished to be a vital force in the realm of private
ideals and convictions. He considered that only which
persuades the understanding to good to be of an exalted
nature. Slavery of every form is identical with evil, but
the slavery of the mind is the most degrading of all tyranny. Bad men, he says, seek

to fetter, not only the bodies but the minds of men, who labour to
introduce into the state the worst of all tyrannies, the tyranny of
their own depraved habits and pernicious opinions.

Eve was indeed adorned with the majesty of beauty and
every outward grace and charm; but all this was vanity
and yielded decisively to Adam's intellectual superiority: •

> For what admir'st thou, what transports thee so,
> An outside? fair no doubt, and worthy well
> Thy cherishing, thy honouring and thy love,
> Not thy subjection: weigh her with thyself,
> Then value. . . . .

These are but a few of many statements of this principle
of individual morality.

The fourth doctrine of Milton's ethics relating to the
individual specifically is the need and value of self-discipline. Man's great foe is not to be found outside himself,
but within. Milton forever insists upon the right of the
individual to be free from any kind of outward con-
straint; his whole life was a constant battle against medievalism to procure freedom for the individual; this,
however, certainly does not imply that he is not to be

governed by unbending law. The law of God, says Milton, is

now written by the Spirit in the hearts of believers. . . . . It is expected of [Christians] that they should be more perfect than those under the law. . . . . The only difference is, that Moses imposes the letter, or the external law, even on those who are not willing to receive it; whereas Christ writes the inward law of God by his spirit on the hearts of believers.

Reason, which is law, must dominate over irrational impulse, or passion:

> Yet he who reigns within himself and rules
> Passions, Desires, and Fears, is more a King;
> Which every wise and vertuous man attains;
> And who attains not, ill aspires to rule
> Cities of men, or head-strong Multitudes,
> Subject himself to Anarchy within
> Or lawless passions in him, which he serves.

The principle of self-discipline is illustrated by a concrete application to Cromwell:

In a short time he almost surpassed the greatest generals in the magnitude and the rapidity of his achievements. Nor is this surprising; for he was a soldier disciplined to perfection in the knowledge of himself. He had either extinguished, or by habit had learned to subdue, the whole host of vain hopes, fears, and passions, which infest the soul. He first acquired the government of himself, and over himself acquired the most signal victories.

The last doctrine in Milton's system of private ethics deals with the moral and practical effects which ensue when passion defeats and dethrones reason.[29] Such a defeat occurred in the minds of Adam and Eve when they

[29] Cf. what Denis Saurat has made of this matter in his *La Pensée de Milton*, as well as in his later and superior *Milton, Man and Thinker*.

fell: Eve was charmed by flattery; she desired to gain
more power, to become a goddess; she wished to rule
over her husband; Adam was "fondly overcome with
Femal charm." Their passions destroyed their reason,
and made them "destitute and bare of all their vertue";
and with it fled their freedom and happiness simultaneously:

> Love was not in thir looks, either to God
> Or to each other, but apparent guilt,
> And shame, and perturbation, and despaire,
> Anger, and obstinacie, and hate, and guile.

The peace and equanimity of their minds had departed:

> For Understanding rul'd not, and the Will
> Heard not her lore, both in subjection now
> To sensual Appetite, who, from beneathe,
> Usurping over sovran Reason, claimd
> Superior sway.

Good men are under the control of the strictest rational
law; they do nothing which, when everything is considered, may result in evil. But bad men know no law whatever—they act according to chance, obeying the impulses that draw them hither and thither, never deterred
by consequences which may be foreseen. Irrational
choice results in the utmost confusion. Such was the
state of Adam and Eve after their fall:

> Nor onely Teares
> Raind at thir Eyes, but high Winds worse within
> Began to rise, high Passions, Anger, Hate,
> Mistrust, Suspicion, Discord and shook sore
> Thir inward State of Mind, calme Region once
> And full of Peace, now tost and turbulent.

Man is the monarch of his own little microcosm, but he had better be a strong and inexorable ruler!

Thus we see that extreme lawlessness and misery are the first results of allowing passion to overcome the reason; but the second consequence is that one who is a thrall to internal despotism soon becomes a slave to an external tyrant also; the latter degradation, however, is merely the inevitable result of the former. The Lady in *Comus*, because she maintained her personal integrity, was proof to all assaults from without. Thus all slavery must, in the last analysis, be the nemesis of inward corruption. And this doctrine applies not only to individuals but to nations as well.

It usually happens by the appointment, and as it were, the retributive justice of the Deity, that that people which cannot govern themselves, and moderate their passions, but crouch under the slavery of their lusts, should be delivered up to the sway of those whom they abhor, and made to submit to an involuntary servitude.

> Yet sometimes Nations will decline so low
> From vertue, which is reason, that no wrong,
> But Justice, and some fatal curse annext
> Deprives them of thir outward libertie,
> Thir inward lost.[30]

Behind Milton's external opposition to Puritanism and behind the practical teachings we have just noticed lie certain fundamental ethical conceptions which constitute general social laws, and which are the vital force

[30] Cf. also *P. W.*, I, 295.

behind everything else. In Milton an assertive rationalism and individualism are everywhere rampant; but the
living force which supports and impregnates them is the
principle of internality. It is by virtue of these that the
essential Milton is everything that the typical Puritan
is not.

It might be well to define our terms. By "rationalism" I mean that attitude of mind which seeks not a particular truth, but Truth; which accepts nothing because
it was believed in the past. Unlike the Puritan, the rationalist considers human reason sacred. And, unlike
the legalist, he never commits himself to a foregone
conclusion: what we now hold to be most sacred may
be most false in the light of pure reason, which is the
only final criterion. Rationalism holds, furthermore, that
there must be change and progress, that without these
life stagnates into corruption and death.

No one can read Milton without observing the practical expression of his rationalism; it is frequently stated
and everywhere implied. He declares

> The gift of reason has been implanted in all. . . . . Reason
> [is] the best arbitrator, the law of law itself. . . . . No law can
> be fundamental but that which is grounded on the light of nature
> or right reason, commonly called the moral law.

This fundamental law, of course, we all possess; and by
it we must be guided. The uncomprehending acceptance
of any doctrine seemed to Milton a gross defection from
duty. He exclaims:

There be, who knows not there be? of protestants and professors, who live and die in as errant and implicit faith, as any lay papist of Loretto.

But "Implicit faith," he declares in the *Christian Doctrine,* " . . . . cannot possibly be genuine faith." In another place he sees in Protestantism a worse tyranny[31] over conscience (individual reason) than in the Roman Catholic Church because, in the former, one man, against his own professed doctrine, enthralls the minds of others; whereas in the latter it is the collective authority of tradition which, in accordance with its avowed principles, forces the individual to conform.

The bibliolatry of the Reformation made Milton's attitude toward scripture the greatest test of his rationalism; but even here we find that he has the courage of his convictions. He draws his doctrine, he says indeed, "from the Holy Scriptures alone."[32] And, seeming to abandon his self-dependence, he continues: "Let us then discard reason in sacred matters, and follow Holy Scripture exclusively." Yet before long we find him maintaining, in a manner which Cheynell would have considered unutterably abominable, that

Under the Gospel, we possess, as it were, a two-fold Scripture; one external, which is the written word, and the other internal, which is the Holy Spirit, written in the hearts of believers. . . . . The written word, I say, of the New Testament, has been liable to frequent corruption, and . . . . has been corrupted. . . . . But the Spirit which leads to truth cannot be corrupted, neither is it easy to deceive a man who is really spiritual.

[31] *Of True Religion, Heresy, Schism, Toleration,* etc. (1674).
[32] *P. W.,* IV, 11.

The historical books of the Old Testament, says Milton, "appear sometimes to contradict themselves on points of chronology." And, therefore, "Everything is to be finally referred to the Spirit, and the unwritten word," which, of course, is man's innate reason.

This doctrine Milton proceeds to apply to scriptural interpretation. Whatever seems irrational he explains away, by one method or another, just as the Socinians did. The doctrine of creation out of nothing he declares false on the basis of metaphysical reasoning.[33] The statement of Christ that Moses permitted divorce because of "hardness of heart" he declares absurd because it is impossible that the bondage under the Gospel should be worse than that under the law: Christ was simply answering the Pharisees according to their folly.[34] Milton arbitrarily refused to see the obvious meaning in the burning of which Paul speaks when he recommends celibacy. In truth, Milton found in scripture only what his reason told him was right.

Milton's many arguments were appeals to reason, and not to authority.[35] It is true that he had studied both the Fathers and the later theologians, and that he was a

[33] *Ibid.*, pp. 177–78.

[34] *Ibid.*, III, 380–401.

[35] Bacon allowed his reason free play in matters scientific; but he was slavishly orthodox in all things political or religious. Milton's was a mind far more courageous and little less original than Bacon's; Milton applied the inductive method, in the broadest possible way, to great and living issues in such a way as to discredit the accepted, and to establish religious, social, and political principles then regarded as heinously subversive but now called simply "modern."

wide scholar in various fields. But he pored over the records of the past, not that he might, like Prynne, compel the present and the future to remain stagnant, but that he might combat his orthodox enemies. He abhorred, he said, "to club quotations with men whose learning and belief lies in marginal stuffings." He believed that every good author makes a personal contribution; he must draw upon his own reason to persuade that of others. He must "teach with authority, which is the life of teaching"; he must "be a doctor in his book." This is the ideal of the *Areopagitica*. To write worthily, a man must not repeat such "common stuff" as is "vulgarly received already," but must reveal some great and new "truth, for the want of which whole nations fare the worse." He must

summon up all his reason and deliberation to assist him; he searches, meditates, is industrious . . . . after . . . . which . . . . he takes himself to be informed in what he writes, as well as any that wrote before him. . . . . A good book is the precious life-blood of a master-spirit, embalmed and treasured up on purpose to a life beyond life.

It contains the "purest efficacy and extraction of living intellect"; it cannot be an appeal to authority but an appeal to reason. Thus it is that "he who destroys a good book, kills reason itself, kills the image of God." In "the mansion house of liberty" there are men "sitting by studious lamps, musing, searching, revolving new notions and ideas; . . . . others as fast reading, trying all things, assenting to the force of reason and convincement." The works of the Puritans are appeals to authority and man's sense of sin; the *Areopagitica* is an appeal to reason, to man's sense of independence and potential virtue.

And it is in this pamphlet, as we should expect, that we find expressed the great rationalistic principles of Milton's thought; the following is a central point: truth must be progressive, not final; and every one must draw his convictions from himself.

Truth is compared in scripture to a streaming fountain; if her waters flow not in a perpetual progression, they sicken into a muddy pool of conformity and tradition.[36]

If a man differ in conviction from his fellows, he should publish his own opinions:

What can be more fair, than when a man judicious, learned . . . . openly by writing, publish to the world what his opinion is, what his reasons, and wherefore that which is now thought cannot be sound?

New truth is necessary to all forward movement; but the dogmatist, of course, clings to, and depends upon, the past:

It [licensing] hinders and retards the importation of our richest merchandise,—truth; . . . . It is not denied, but gladly confessed, we are to send our thanks and vows to heaven, louder than most of nations, for that great measure of truth which we

[36] Milton's hatred for custom, which he considered synonymous with error, he expressed again and again. "Hence it is that error supports custom, custom countenances error; and these two between them would persecute and chase away all truth and solid wisdom out of human life" (*P. W.*, III, 172).

enjoy . . . . but he who thinks we . . . . have attained the utmost prospect of reformation that the mortal glass wherein we contemplate can shew us . . . . by this very opinion declares that he is yet far short of truth. . . . . The light which we have gained was given us, not to be ever staring on, but by it to discover onward things more remote from our knowledge. It is not the unfrocking of a priest, the unmitring of a bishop, and the removing him from off the presbyterian shoulders, that will make us a happy nation: no; if other things as great in the church, and in the rule of life both economical and political, be not looked into and reformed, we have looked so long upon the blaze that Zuinglius and Calvin have beaconed up to us, that we are stark blind. . . . . To be still searching what we know not, by what we know; still closing up truth to truth as we find it, (for all her body is homogeneal and proportional,) this is the golden rule in theology as well as in arithmetic.

As yet, then, we have made but a small beginning in our progress; and endless changes lie ahead, each of which will to some extent repudiate the past.

The rationalist (contrast his method with Prynne's) loves to meet his foe in the open field where human reason grapples with human reason, where it cannot be choked with authority and stifled unheard:

Let her and falsehood grapple: who ever knew truth put to the worse, in a free and open encounter? Her confuting is the best and surest suppressing. . . . . For who knows not that truth is strong, next to the Almighty; she needs no policies, nor stratagems, nor licensings to make her victorious, those are the shifts and the defences that error uses against her power: give her but room, and do not bind her when she sleeps.

This is Milton's demand:

Give me the liberty to know, to utter, and to argue freely according to conscience, above all liberties.

Milton's rationalism and repudiation of Puritan dogma are perhaps most boldly declared in the *Christian Doctrine,* where he denies the validity of the Trinitarian conception because it is supra-rational;[37] and most philosophically in his proof of God's existence, where he says that man's possession of reason is final evidence that a good power pervades and dominates the universe.[38]

We have now before us a brief abstract of Milton's rationalism, which expresses clearly and vigorously one phase of his modernity. His second great conception in general ethics is that of individualism. By "individualism" I mean that philosophy which demands rights for each of us; which, indeed, places the interest of the individuals before that of the group. It postulates the right of each human being to have his own opinions, doctrines, judgments—in short, to live his life independently as far as this is possible. Individualism is the enemy of uniformity and of conformity to accepted standards. Rationalism and individualism are, of course, the most uncompromising enemies of medieval Christianity; and they are characteristic of present-day thinking. Milton's doctrine of individuality harmonizes completely with his rationalism. It is manifest in the *Doctrine and Discipline* (1643): if the individual finds himself miserable in his domestic relationship, the marriage tie is to be dissolved. We find it in the tractate on education (1644): the process of education must go on until the student "shall be thus fraught with an universal insight into things," that is, until he becomes pre-eminently able to form in-

[37] *Ibid.,* IV, 95.   [38] *Ibid.,* p. 15.

dividual, valid generalizations. It is given us in the *Tenure* (1649): kings are not representatives of God, but of the people, and subject to their laws. It is proclaimed in the *Christian Doctrine* (1658?): every man must make his own religion. It is courageously expressed in the pamphlet *Of True Religion*, etc. (1673), in which, putting all Protestants upon the same basis, he argues successively in favor of toleration for all the persecuted sects. All have an equal right to their opinions; no one has any right to compel in matters of conviction. Thus we find Milton's startlingly modern individualism expressed in every aspect of his thinking and during every period of his life; and in every expression of it he was diametrically opposed to the Puritans.

But for the philosophical exposition we must turn again to the *Areopagitica*. Lack of individualism implies conformity: and conformity implies stagnation and death. The following is spoken specifically of the Puritans:

These are the fruits which a dull ease and cessation of our knowledge will bring forth among the people. How goodly, and how to be valued were such an obedient unanimity as this! What a fine conformity would it starch us all into! Doubtless a staunch and solid piece of framework, as any January could freeze together. . . . . This is the golden rule in theology as well as in arithmetic, and makes up the best harmony in a church; not the forced and outward union of cold, and neutral, and inwardly divided minds.

Milton expressed a fierce hatred for "the discipline of Geneva, formed and fabricated already to our hands," which left neither privilege nor responsibility to the individual. This discipline, of course, was Presbyterianism or English Puritanism. Sects and schisms are necessary, being the expression of individual attitude and conscience; and we must never try to compel others to our own opinions;[39] there should be a general and internal unity in infinite variety—neither uniformity nor conformity:

Where there is much desire to learn, there of necessity will be much arguing, much writing, many opinions; for opinion in good men is but knowledge in the making. Under these fantastic terrors of sect and schism, we wrong the earnest and zealous thirst after knowledge and understanding. . . . . What some lament of, we rather should rejoice at. . . . . Could we but forego this prelatical tradition of crowding free consciences and Christian liberties into canons and precepts of men. . . . . I fear yet this iron yoke of outward conformity hath left a slavish print upon our necks. . . . . We do not see that while we still affect by all means a rigid external formality, we may as soon fall again into a gross conforming stupidity, a stark and dead congealment of "wood and hay and stubble" forced and frozen together, which is more to the sudden degenerating of a church than many subdichotomies of petty schisms.

Not that I can think well of every light separation. . . . . Yet if all cannot be of one mind, as who looks they should be? this doubtless is more wholesome, more prudent, and more Christian, that many be tolerated rather than all compelled.

That these doctrines and that this philosophy and attitude of mind were, by reason of their modernity and

[39] It is upon this point, of course, that modern life is chiefly to be differentiated from medieval.

uniqueness, most extraordinary and revolutionary in 1645, is a fact which even the most casual student of the sixteenth and seventeenth centuries must recognize at once. We naturally expect some great principle in Milton's own thinking to lie behind all this, and such is the fact.

It is convenient to call this the "doctrine of internality." It is a concept that sees in the individual the source of all moral reality and intellectual power. To the Puritan, man was a complete nullity except in his power to commit sin. But, according to Milton's doctrine, no external existence has any ethical valuation. The mind, by developing its own resources, can make itself impregnable to all assaults from without. We must depend upon ourselves and develop our internal resources. Everything that is of any significance is in our own power. Every man is the lord of his own fate. It is in this that Milton most completely repudiates Puritanism and all that it implies. Man must, accordingly, look to himself —never to any external or supernal power—for the formation of his convictions and the guidance of his conduct. Milton's rationalism and individualism are the direct outgrowth of his principle of internality.

This principle, which I believe to be the animating force behind all his thought and action, is expressed again and again; it is stated most completely in *Comus,* in the *Areopagitica,* and, with certain modifications, in *Paradise Lost* and *Paradise Regained*. Although, as expressed in his poetry, this conception is imaginative, Mil-

ton translated it into action in his prose and in his life.
It is the theme of *Comus:*

> Vertue could see to do what vertue would
> By her own radiant light, though Sun and Moon
> Were in the flat Sea sunk.

> He that has light within his own clear breast
> May sit i' the centre, and enjoy bright day;
> But he that hides a dark soul and foul thoughts
> Benighted walks under the mid-day Sun;
> Himself is his own dungeon.

> So dear to Heav'n is Saintly chastity,
> That, when a soul is found sincerely so,
> A thousand liveried Angels lackey her
> Driving far off each thing of sin and guilt
> And in cleer dream and solemn vision
> Tell her of things that no gross ear can hear;
> Till oft converse with heavenly habitants
> Begin to cast a beam on th' outward shape,
> The unpolluted temple of the mind,
> And turns it by degrees to the souls essence
> Till all be made immortal.[40]

[40] Let us realize that Milton's opposition to Puritanism and his abhorrence of the profligacy of the Restoration were equally great. The
Puritans suppressed all natural human impulses, and these Milton considered good; the court of Charles II allowed every lewd passion unex-
ampled indulgence, and this Milton fiercely condemned. Cf. *P. L.,* I,
492–502. Neither the Puritans nor the Cavaliers saw in the mind a possible citadel of impregnable virtue. Both, furthermore, were slavish in
their attitude toward established theory—the Puritan in religion, the
Cavalier in government. On philosophical and practical grounds, Milton attacked every essential principle governing the lives of the two
great classes of his contemporaries.

This I hold firm:
Vertue may be assail'd, but never hurt,
Surpriz'd by unjust force, but not enthrall'd;
Yea, even that which Mischief meant most harm
Shall in the happy trial prove most glory.

My sister is not so defenceless left
As you imagine; she has a hidden strength
Which you remember not.
  Sec. Bro. What hidden strength,
Unless the strength of Heav'n, if you mean that?[41]

  Eld. Bro. I mean that too, but yet a hidden strength,
Which, if Heav'n gave it, may be term'd her own;
'Tis Chastity, my brother, chastity;[42]
She that has that is clad in compleat steel.[43]

[41] The Elder Brother is, of course, Milton's spokesman in *Comus*. He represents the principle of internality; the Second Brother represents the Puritan philosophy, the idea that the individual must depend upon external forces for salvation.

[42] Do not confuse Milton's "chastity" with mere sexual continence or abstinence; it is a much broader term, and implies all that the Stoic doctrine of internality does.

[43] This seems as good a place as any to call attention to one more important fact related to the principle of internality. We find this reflected in Milton's ideal of Christ, especially in his "Ode on the Morning of Christ's Nativity," written when Milton was very young, as well as in *Paradise Regained,* the product of late maturity. In the latter, we find that it is Christ the exemplar, the conqueror of human temptations, who is stressed—not the Christ who saves mankind through his vicarious atonement on the Cross. Milton everywhere stresses the intellectual, not the suffering, Saviour. And in the "Ode" the conquering Son of God is even more in evidence; he knows nothing of humility or self-abnegation, he is not a man of sorrows, acquainted with grief. Rather, he is the war god, who, with furious attack, drives all the usurping gods to their dens and caves where they may hide. He is "That glorious

From the passages quoted several facts are evident, all bearing on the same principle and all serving to contrast Milton with Puritanism: first, virtue is an all-powerful thing and exists within the mind, is its own intrinsic and inexpugnable possession, derived from no source outside itself; second, the hidden strength, chastity—which, with Milton, simply meant physical and intellectual purity—is not given man by heaven, but is his own gift to himself; third, internality is so pervasive a thing that only those who are pure in mind can receive excellent things through the senses; fourth, this inward purity, bestowed by man upon himself, is so dynamic in its powers that it achieves for him, unaided by any external power, the conversion of the body, the "unpolluted temple of the mind," to spirituality and to immortality in bliss, perfection, and glory.

The *Areopagitica*, which, even though in prose, is semi-imaginative, explains the doctrine more methodically; the profit which a man may derive from any external thing of whatever kind depends not at all upon the nature of the object but upon the quality of the mind:

And he might have added another remarkable saying of the same author: "To the pure all things are pure;" not only meats and drinks, but all kind of knowledge, whether of good or evil; the knowledge cannot defile, nor consequently the books, if the will and conscience be not defiled. For books are as meats and

---

Form, that Light unsufferable," before which "The Oracles are dumb" and the pagan gods cower in trembling fear. In order to realize the contrast, read Crashaw's ode on the same subject. Here Christ is the "meek Majesty, soft King."

viands are; some of good, some of evil substance. . . . . Wholesome meats to a vitiated stomach differ little or nothing from un-
wholesome; and best books to a naughty mind are not unapplica-
ble to occasions of evil. Bad meats will scarce breed good nourishment in the healthiest concoction; but herein the difference is of
bad books, that they to a discreet and judicious reader serve in
many respects to discover, to confute, to forewarn, and to illustrate. . . . . All opinions, yea, errors, known, read, and collated,
are of main service and assistance toward the speedy attainment
of what is truest. . . . . A wise man, like a good refiner, can gath-
er gold out of the drossiest volume, and . . . . a fool will be a
fool with the best book, yea, or without a book; there is no reason
that we should deprive a wise man of any advantage to his wisdom, while we seek to restrain from a fool that which being re-
strained will be no hinderance to his folly. . . . . A wise man will
make better use of an idle pamphlet, than a fool will do of sacred
scripture.

In the world, good and evil are very much the same:

Good and evil we know in the field of this world grow up together almost inseparably; and the knowledge of good is . . . .
involved and interwoven with the knowledge of evil. . . . . It was
from out the rind of one apple tasted, that the knowledge of good
and evil, as two twins cleaving together, leaped forth into the
world. And perhaps this is that doom which Adam fell into of
knowing good and evil; that is to say, of knowing good by evil.

Victory over real temptation is the only proof of virtue; and, in opposition to the Puritan, Milton considered
virtue and action inseparable:

He that can apprehend and consider vice with all her baits
and seeming pleasures, and yet abstain, and yet distinguish, and
yet prefer that which is truly better, he is the true warfaring
Christian. I cannot praise a fugitive and cloistered virtue, unexer-

cised and unbreathed, that never sallies out and seeks her adversary, but slinks out of the race where that immortal garland is to
be run for, not without heat and dust. . . . . That virtue, therefore, which is but a youngling in the contemplation of evil, and
knows not the utmost that vice promises to her followers, and re-
jects it, is but a blank virtue, not a pure; her whiteness is but an
excremental whiteness.

We must use the good within the mind to judge the
appearances of the world:

Since therefore the knowledge and survey of vice is in this
world so necessary to the constituting of human virtue, and the
scanning of error to the confirmation of truth, how can we more
safely, and with less danger, scout into the regions of sin and falsity, than by reading all manner of tractates, and hearing all manner
of reason?

The following is fundamental. Vice and virtue are
personal, intrinsic, internal, existing quite irrespective of
anything external to the mind:

Wherefore did he [God] create passions within us, pleasures
round about us, but that these rightly tempered are the very ingre-
dients of virtue? They are not skilful considerers of human things,
who imagine to remove sin by removing the matter of sin; . . . .
and when this is done, yet the sin remains entire. Though ye take
from a covetous man all his treasure, he has yet one jewel left, ye
cannot bereave him of his covetousness. Banish all objects of lust,
shut up all youth into the severest discipline that can be exercised
in any hermitage, ye cannot make them chaste, that came not
hither so. . . . .

Suppose we could expel sin by this means; look how much we
thus expel of sin, so much we expel of virtue: for the matter of
them both is the same: remove that, and ye remove them both
alike.

When Milton wrote *Paradise Lost,* he had undergone many experiences; he had become a Christian of a kind. Yet his principle of internality remained essentially unchanged, and is expressed repeatedly:

> The mind is its own place and in it self
> Can make a Heav'n of Hell, a Hell of Heav'n.

This principle is inexorably valid, as Satan discovers to his sorrow:

> Me miserable! which way shall I flie
> Infinite wrauth and Infinite despaire?
> Which way I fly is Hell; my self am Hell;
> And in the lowest deep, a lower deep
> Still threatning to devour me opens wide,
> To which the Hell I suffer seems a Heav'n.

Christ attains excellence because he achieves that rational mastery of himself which is Milton's ethical ideal:

> Yet he who reigns within himself, and rules
> Passions, Desires, and Fears, is more a King;
> Which every wise and vertuous man attains.

That this rationalism, this individualism, and, most of all, this principle of internality are not only diametrically opposed to Puritanism but also remarkably in consonance with modern thought must be obvious. This is by no means all the evidence which Milton's works afford in support of our thesis, but it is sufficient.

Only one more fact remains to be established in the present chapter—the origin of Milton's great ethical ideal. Are we to look for it in some Renaissance thinker?[44] But the Renaissance did not develop any great or original system of morality—it was too much interested in other things: in life, action, metaphysics—and cared little about the problem of conduct, which is acute only when life has grown relatively corrupt and men are compelled to seek consciously for happiness. Or did Milton originate his own ethical system? But all evidence tends to show that his was not the creative, but the absorbing and disseminative type of mind. He had no quiet contemplative years at his disposal to bring into existence new ideas and systems. He was abreast of his time and

[44] It will not do, here, to forget the fact of Milton's debt to Spenser, which has already been pointed out by Professor Edwin Greenlaw. In the *Areopagitica* we read of the "sage and serious poet Spenser, (whom I dare be known to think a better teacher than Scotus or Aquinas,) describing true temperance under the form of Guion, [and] bring[ing] him in with his palmer through the cave of Mammon, and the bower of earthly bliss, that he might see and know, and yet abstain."

Spenser's imaginative, ethical principle is undoubtedly an idealized rendition of the Aristotelian Golden Mean, colored by Renaissance enthusiasm. The idea that those who are pure in heart and in mind and who overcome every internal evil are impregnable to all assault from without is the underlying teaching of the *Faerie Queene*. We need not doubt that Spenser's conceptions of Una, Guyon, and Britomart were active in Milton's mind when he composed *Comus,* in which the lady is a kind of synthesis of these three creations.

Nevertheless, no one can read both the teacher and the greater pupil without realizing that Milton's ethics are deeper, more philosophical, and more practical than Spenser's. In Milton, we find more knowledge, both of philosophy and of life, with its vital, human issues. His teaching indicates a profound grasp of that whole aspect of pagan thinking which culminated in Stoicism. Concerning Spenser such a statement can scarcely be made.

formulated the most advanced doctrines and applied them to current problems; but he did not create conceptions.

It is necessary, then, that we look for a source; and a clue to it is not far to seek. As we learn from many passages taken from works written during various periods of his life, Milton had a great and very conscious admiration for Greek culture, learning, and philosophy. Comus is made to condemn the Stoics, which, of course, is an expression of Milton's admiration for them. Milton's abundant use of mythological allusion, which constitutes an intrinsic part of his poetry, is further evidence of his love for pagan culture. In his treatise on Christian doctrine, Milton refers nine times to the Greek writers of tragedy, considering them authorities on moral problems. Aristotle he calls "one of the best interpreters of nature and morality." He speaks of the "divine volumes of Plato and his equal Xenophon." Concerning his studies at Horton, he says: "I enjoyed an interval of uninterrupted leisure, which I entirely devoted to the perusal of the Greek and Latin classics." In the *Animadversions* we read: "The heathen philosophers thought that virtue was for its own sake inestimable, and the greatest gain of a teacher to make a soul virtuous." Marcus Aurelius, Milton calls "that mirror of princes." Milton's school was consciously modeled upon those of Plato, Aristotle, Pythagoras, and Isocrates, and the studies to be pursued in it were the classics, of which the crowning glory was to consist of treatises on morality.[45] In the *Areopagitica* he expresses great reverence for "Hellenic learning."

Thus we are led to expect that we must look among the moral philosophers of Greece and Rome for the source of Milton's great ethical principle. It is not, however, among those whom he mentions most frequently—Plato, Aristotle, Xenophon, Plutarch, and Cicero—that we are to seek its ultimate formulation. As usual, Milton found it necessary to refer least to those with whom he was most in accord.

Socrates was the first great philosopher among the Greeks who attempted to solve the problem of human conduct and happiness. He gave it a rationalistic and intellectualistic treatment which all his successors also pursued. He made virtue and happiness a matter of the mind. With him ignorance and evil were identical; and virtue and happiness on the one hand were synonymous with knowledge and wisdom on the other. That virtue could be obtained only through the exercise of reason and knowledge was clear to Socrates, but the precise method he could never adequately explain. The reason for the endless, unmerciful, and insoluble enigmas of this dialectician was the impossibility, under which he labored, of declaring ultimately what virtue and happiness consist in. The difficulty with the Socratic system was that in it virtue and happiness depend upon contingencies, upon external and material factors, at least to some extent. For Socrates (as well as for Plato, Xeno-

[45] Cf. *Of Education*.

phon, Aristotle, and Plutarch) material existences possess intrinsic value, and human happiness must be considered in relation to them. "Sickness is an evil? Beyond a doubt."[46] There is a certain materialistic utilitarianism in this. Because of the indefinability of virtue, human happiness was an unteachable science. Socrates was groping in comparative darkness. As long as we make virtue, happiness—the good—dependent upon pleasure and pain, which are mere sensations, there can be no satisfactory formulation of moral principles.

In Aristotle we find a development indeed of the problem laid down by Socrates, but no answer. The same intellectualistic eudaemonism is present.[47] Happiness and virtue are to be gained through self-control; reason must rule over passion; understanding must direct the will to pursue that which, when everything has been considered, is seen to be of the greatest value.

The Hellenic moral philosophers saw that all happiness must depend upon the freedom of the will, for where there is no choice of action, there can be no rational happiness. Their study was, then, to find how the will *could be most free*. It was the solution of that problem which first produced the doctrine of internality.

During the period 400 B.C. to 100 A.D. the civilization of Greece and Rome consummated a materialistic development which made the problem of morality exceedingly acute. The brutality, sensuality, obscenity,

[46] *Socratic Discourses*, "Everyman Series," II, 223.

[47] Cf. *Nicomachean Ethics*, "Everyman Series," p. 54.

and consequent nausea in Nero's capital quite surpass
our power of imagination. The world was flooded with
a "literature of despair." Life seemed quite hopeless.
Men were in the condition that follows the repulsion consequent upon oversatiety in debauchery. They had ex-
hausted the possibilities of pleasing the physical; where
should they turn for satisfaction now?

We have already spoken of the two solutions—
Christianity and Stoicism—which were offered to remedy the evil in the clutches of which life was disintegrating. These are similar and present a radical departure
from the thinking of Socrates, Plato, and Aristotle in
that they deny all intrinsic valuation to material things.
All that any one can desire in this world—riches, honor,
glory, health, friends, etc.—are, in themselves, worthless. But the Christian, in that he looks above and beyond whence his help cometh, is diametrically opposed
to the Stoic; he "desires a better country, that is an
heavenly." Christ said:

> He that loveth his life shall lose it; and he that hateth his life
> in this world shall keep it unto life eternal. He that believeth on
> the Son shall have everlasting life. In my Father's house are
> many mansions; if it were not so, I would have told you. I go to
> prepare a place for you. . . . . I am the way, the truth, and the
> life; no man cometh to the Father, but by me.

This was the message of Christianity to the world: ne-
gate yourself, hate this world and the life thereof, surrender to the unseen, believe in Christ, put yourself in
the right relationship with the supernatural, and you will

go to Heaven after death; refuse this invitation and you will spend eternity in hell-fire. It was out of this that Augustinianism inevitably grew. It made the unseen glorious by pouring contempt upon the seen. The message of Stoicism was quite different. Marcus Aurelius says:

> Look within; within is the fountain of good, and it will ever bubble up, if thou wilt only ever dig.

> Be like the promontory against which the waves continually break, but it stands firm and tames the fury of the waters around it.[48]

The message of Stoicism was this: Depend upon your reason and knowledge to gain virtue; develop your own resources; as there is no life after this, don't worry about the future; gain happiness from the consciousness of right-doing; make yourself absolutely independent of all things external to yourself; derive all good from within; as material things are only appearances and not within your power, accept them or resign them without emotion as fate or fortune may dictate; free yourself from all passion and achieve happiness by desiring those things only which you can at all times bestow upon yourself in any condition of life.

This is Stoicism, the doctrine of internality. Zeno, whose writings are not extant, was the founder of the school. The same philosophy was expounded by the slave Epictetus in his *Discourses,* and by the Emperor Aurelius in his *Meditations.* It was systematically set forth by the philosopher Seneca. It is in the works of

[48] *Meditations.*

Epictetus, Aurelius, and Seneca that we find the source
of Milton's great ethical ideal. I wish to quote a few
passages—sufficient to indicate that the morality of
Comus and the *Areopagitica* is inspired by Stoicism.
Note that Milton's statement that the materials of both
vice and virtue are the same is the Stoic doctrine of "appearances."

The indifferent are the things which lie between the virtues
and the vices,—wealth, health, life, death, pleasure, pain. . . . .
I have this purpose—to make you free from restraint. . . . .
Neither wealth is in our power, nor health, nor reputation, nor, in
a word, anything else except the right use of appearances.[49] Death
and life, and honour and dishonour, pain and pleasure—all these
things happen equally to good men and bad, being things which
made us neither better nor worse. Therefore, they are neither
good nor evil.[50] Thank the gods that they have allowed you to be
above those things which they have not placed in your power. . . . .
For what, then, have the gods made you accountable? For that
which is alone in your power, the proper use of appearances.[51]

The inviolability of the happiness resulting from
virtue is thus explained by Seneca and Aurelius:

Virtue . . . . makes the prisoner . . . . happier than the ex-
ecutioner and sickness better than health. . . . . Virtue is that
perfect good which is the complement of a happy life. . . . . It is
the knowledge both of others and itself, it is an invincible greatness of mind, not to be elevated or dejected with good or ill fortune. . . . . It is virtue alone that raises us above griefs, hopes,
fears. . . . . A good man is happy with himself and independent
of fortune.[52]

[49] Epictetus. [51] Epictetus.
[50] Aurelius. [52] Seneca, *Morals* (London, 1803), Vol. I.

Remember that the ruling faculty is invincible. . . . . Therefore the mind that is free from passions is a citadel, for man has
nothing more secure to which he can fly for refuge and for the
future be inexpugnable.[53] The good man is invincible . . . . take
his land: take his slaves, his magisterial office, take his poor body.
. . . . The only contest into which he enters is that about things
which are within the power of his will; how then will he not be
invincible?[54]

This reads like a prose version of *Comus;* and the fact is
that *Comus* is simply a poetic rendition of this. The happiness which is the result of virtue is an inviolable possession.

According to the Stoic—as is implied in the preceding quotations—there are two great classes of existences in the moral world—those which are in the power
of the will and those which are not. It is in our power to
assume whatever attitude we will toward externals, and
to assume the right one will lead to freedom and happiness. The good man is he who is absolutely without perturbations of soul; who, regarding all external things
with utter indifference, centers all his attention on reason and virtue. The bad man is he who allows his desires for, or fear of, external things to influence his mind.
For example, the man who flatters to gain a high position, who lies to gain wealth, who cringes in the prospect
of death, or who is overcome by grief at any loss, is sunk
in a life of passion—external things intrude themselves
into his mind. The following expresses a portion of the
Stoic ideal:

[53] Aurelius.   [54] Epictetus.

Who then is invincible? It is he whom none of the things
disturb which are independent of the will. . . . . If you should
throw money in his way, he will despise it. Well, suppose you put
a young girl in his way, what then? and what if it is in the dark?
. . . . and what if it should be praise; and what if it should be
death? He is able to overcome all. . . . . He will still conquer.
This is my invincible athlete.[55]

Let us now, finally, quote a few passages which express in the clearest terms the Stoics' doctrine of internality; this is the source of all their teachings and principles. It is expressed in multiform diversity and ani-
mates almost every thought which they formulated—
externals are accidental and unreal; the mind is the sole
reality:

He is poor who has need of another, and has not from himself
all things which are useful for life. . . . . Suppose that men kill
thee, cut thee in pieces, curse thee. What can these things do to
pervert thy mind from remaining pure, wise, sober, just?[56] God
has fixed his law and says, "If you would have anything good, receive it from yourself." . . . . From within comes ruin, and from
within comes help. . . . . If you gape after externals, you must of
necessity ramble up and down in obedience to the will of your
master. And who is your master? He who has the power over the
things which you seek to gain or try to avoid.[57]

The mind is above all fortune; if that be evil, it makes everything else so, too. . . . . There is no defense in walls, fortifica-
tions, and engines against the power of fortune; we must provide
ourselves within, and when we are safe there, we are invincible;
we may be battered, but not taken. . . . . All the good and ill we
do is under the dominion of the mind; . . . . a clear conscience
states us in an inviolable peace; and . . . . the greatest blessing

[55] Epictetus.   [56] Aurelius.   [57] Epictetus.

in nature is that which every man may bestow upon himself. . . . .
No man shall ever be poor, that goes to himself for what he wants,
and that is the readiest way to riches; . . . . shall I call him poor
that wants nothing, though he may be beholden for it to his patience rather than to fortune? or shall any man deny him to be
rich, whose riches can never be taken away? . . . . Let the mind
be great and glorious, and all other things are despicable in comparison.[58]

This is the central principle of Stoicism; and it is also
the actuating doctrine in Milton. The impregnability of
the fortress of virtue and intellect, a personal and individual possession from which all good may proceed, is
the ideal expressed. But just as the human mind is the
source of all good, so is it also the source of all evil.
There only may ethical reality exist. All else is but
shadow, and the material upon which the ruling faculty
—the mind—may exercise its powers.

Milton's essential repudiation of Puritanism and ab-
sorption of essential Stoicism are indeed most significant.
By these actions he is marked chiefly as a man of the
modern world. He is a rationalist, instead of a legalist.
But above all he is an individualist, the destroyer of medieval Realism, uniformity, and conformity; and a powerful herald of that democracy which has made itself
felt in every aspect of human existence—the domestic,
the political, the social, and the religious. His theory
that the human mind can by no moral right be subjected
to external tyranny is the secret of Milton's ethics; this
enabled him to treat with scorn and to revolt against the

[58] Seneca.

great social and religious codes which ruled mankind in
his day. It was because of this that he could proclaim the
validity of divorce and the liberty of the press; that he
could declare kings subject to the laws of the governed;
that, in theology, he could be a universal heretic; and
that, in short, he could have so much in common with
present-day thinking. This principle marks Milton as
perhaps the most significant exponent of the modern theory of life, which holds that all men are inalienably free
and potentially equal, that they can depend upon themselves for everything. It offers a far-reaching solution
for the greatest of all social problems; but, far more than
that, it gives the individual a rational rock of refuge in all
disaster and a satisfying solution for the miserable con-
tradictions of human life. But the final consequences of
the principle have as yet by no means been realized. It
is a doctrine that contains more sublime truth than mediocre common sense; but this truth is one on which may
be founded the happiness and the elevation of the individual; the integrity of societies; the strength of nations;
and the yet unrealized peace and unity of the world.
Such are the potentialities of the doctrine of internality;
and Milton is probably the greatest teacher of ethics
that England has yet produced.[59]

[59] This chapter is the reworking and expansion of an article, to be
published in the *Philological Quarterly*, during 1927, and called "Milton's Essential Relationship to Puritanism and Stoicism."

CHAPTER III

MILTON'S METAPHYSICS

Under the title "Milton's Metaphysics," it may be best to discuss, first, those general metaphysical principles which lie behind all this thinking, both secular and religious, and which he would have held whether he had come into contact with Puritanism or not; and, second, those specific religious doctrines, distinctly metaphysical in their nature, which he developed in his Christian theology and which could not have existed outside that system. Of course, there are points where the line of demarcation between the two is very vague; for example, Milton's conception of God is both secular and religious, as is his conception of the relation between the Infinite and ourselves. Nevertheless, the division is convenient.

GENERAL METAPHYSICAL DOCTRINES

Basic in Milton's metaphysics is his conception of the cosmos. *Paradise Lost* is a cosmical poem, its setting being the universe. It is not certain whether Milton had adopted the Copernican theory or not: but it is certain that he had moved far beyond the Ptolemaic. We read in the *Areopagitica:* "I found and visited the famous Galileo, grown old, a prisoner to the Inquisition, for thinking otherwise in astronomy than the Franciscan and Dominican licensers thought." From this it appears that Milton sympathized with the new astronomy; and we can scarcely doubt that a mind like his would have acquainted itself thoroughly with it. But it is also certain that the framework of the terrestrial universe, as described in *Paradise Lost*, is distinctly Ptolemaic. There is, however, one passage in the poem which seems to give the reader his choice between the geocentric and the heliocentric conceptions—this is the one beginning:

> What if the Sun
> Be centre to the World. . . . .

Milton does not seem to have recognized the myriad suns and circling globes, outside our own little system, which Bruno imagined and of which Galileo proved the existence; nevertheless, Milton's conception of the cosmos was scarcely less vast than theirs. The terrestrial universe of Milton is, indeed, that of Ptolemy, with the permitted alternative of making the sun its center; but, in the old system, the *primum mobile* was the uttermost boundary of all existence; while in Milton's, our little universe, which it bounds, is the merest speck in the whole system of things. In Dante's cosmology, hell and purgatory are both within the circumference of the earth;[1] and the various orders of the blessed dwell in the ten heavens, which are the planets or spheres sur-

[1] There is a very curious phrase in *Paradise Lost* (cf. XII, 42) which assumes hell to be within the earth. How such an anomaly could have crept into the poem is indeed difficult to say.

rounding the earth. But beyond the Empyrean or the tenth heaven, which is enclosed in a hard and opaque shell, there is absolutely no further existence. As Masson says, the medieval theologian-astronomer could put his arm condescendingly around the whole universe and pat it with his hand complacently. It is not so in Milton's cosmology: here neither hell nor heaven is within the *primum mobile*, nor is infinite space there; our universe is but a finite, in fact, an infinitesimal, sphere. In comparison with heaven, it looked to Satan, who was sailing toward it through the abyss, like the smallest of visible stars compared to the moon.

It seems only reasonable to say here that no matter what Milton may personally have believed in regard to astronomy, his system in *Paradise Lost* was probably chosen for the sake of convenience. The astronomy of Copernicus would not do for *Paradise Lost;* it was without the possibility of localization; it was simply an endless cosmos of similarly circling spheres. The infinity of Milton's conception is vague; like his poetic imagery, it is profoundly suggestive and leaves much to the reader's imagination; but in Galileo's system the conception of boundlessness is less indefinite. It is true that the latter was superior as a presentation of scientific truth; but the former was superior for art. Furthermore, we must realize that Milton's message is not at all scientific; but it is supremely artistic, ethical, and philosophical.

Many previous critics of Milton have made dia-

grams to illustrate his cosmos; but, as the student may
have no such aid at hand, we will venture another.

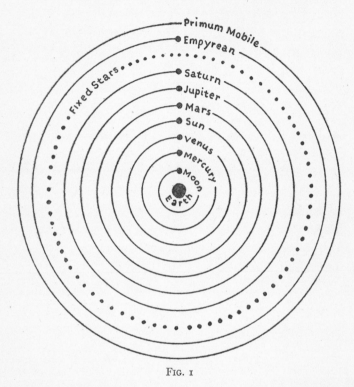

FIG. 1

Figure 1 illustrates the Ptolemaic system, implicitly
followed by Dante, and approximately by Milton.

A word or two of explanation ought, perhaps, to be
added. *Primum mobile* means, of course, "first moved."
Of all the circling spheres it is that first put into motion

and that within which all the rest are moved. The fixed
stars, the sun, and each of the planets, are carried, as
it were, by the shell of a hollow sphere; the circles
shown in the figure are not mere orbit-paths, but trans-
parent solids which support the various bodies revolving about the earth. The sphere of the fixed stars is
that which contains the great majority of the heavenly
lights. The ancient astronomers noticed that these keep
their relative positions, whereas the planets do not.
They were therefore called "the fixed stars," because
they were thought to be fixed in a single shell, all of
which, naturally was equidistant from the central earth.
The crystalline sphere was thought to be a kind of
layer of brilliant liquid light, which, like the planets
within it, circled the earth at an even pace. Ptolemy
thought that the earth stood absolutely still; but Milton, following the modern astronomers in this respect,
accepted not only the teaching that the earth revolves
on its axis but also that this axis is tilted twenty-three
and one-half degrees.[2]

But the epic drama of *Paradise Lost* is played
through not on "this earth, a spot, a grain, an atom,"
but in the whole cosmos, which is illustrated by Figure
2. Milton warns us against considering heaven of a
particular shape: it is "wide in circuit, undetermined
square or round." The terrestrial universe, called the
"World," depends from this by means of a golden

[2] *Ibid.*, X, 668 ff.

chain.[3] The Deep itself, or Chaos, is boundless.[4] And we are told that hell, or the Infernal Pit, which is covered by a great vault, is bottomless.[5] Every aspect of the whole conception implies that the universe is infinite: its extent is simply unimaginable. Nevertheless,

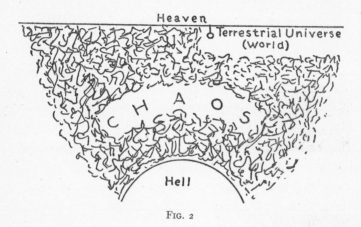

Fig. 2

all of this is not the stage for *Paradise Lost;* the action is centralized, leaving the cosmos to extend itself boundlessly in all directions, where chaos alone exists.

Of course, those within the world can see nothing beyond the *primum mobile.* There is one little aperture in this, however, on the side toward heaven. Sometimes a ladder is let down to it from the Empyrean,[6] a name which Milton gives to heaven. And a ray of light pass-

[3] *Ibid.,* II, 1006, 1051.
[4] *Ibid.,* VII, 168 ff.
[5] *Ibid.,* VI, 866.
[6] *Ibid.,* III, 503, 540.

ing through this opening, penetrates into the darkness about.[7]

This, which is all very simple, is briefly Milton's conception of the more obvious aspects of the physical universe. But behind, there is much more, far more subtle and complex, such as the theories of God, matter, and creation.

Milton's conception of the Deity is the next great metaphysical doctrine to consider. It is impossible that he should have escaped wholly the influence of the orthodox creed, which taught that God consists of three distinct persons—the Father, the Son, and the Holy Ghost—who are all very God of very God, consubstantial with each other, and alike eternal. It is impossible that the author of *Comus* and the *Areopagitica* should so completely have negated his own reason as to accept this dogma; and he did not, saying, like the Socinians, that the word of God, which is the product of universal reason, could not be contrary to the finite or individual reason,[8] which is the image of God.[9]

The fact is that for the trinity of persons Milton substituted a trinity of mode or manifestation.[10] Re-

[7] *Ibid.*, l. 499.   [8] Cf. *Ch. Doct., P. W.*, IV, 95.

[9] *Ibid.*, p. 15. Also *ibid.*, II, 55.

[10] The author has shown elsewhere (*P. M. L. A.*, December, 1926) that Milton's trinitarian conception and many other theological doctrines are strikingly similar to those of Michael Servetus, burned in 1553. The ancient Sabellians and Photinians had taught a modal trinity; but, in comparison with that of Servetus, this was exceedingly

taining a doctrine that scripture could be made to countenance, Milton made it comprehensible to reason, and
such as to enthrall the speculative mind.

---

crude, naïve, and unphilosophical. Giordano Bruno (burned 1600), although he did not apply his metaphysics to theology, as did Servetus,
taught, exactly like both him and Milton, that God is the Infinite, the
Absolute, the One, identical with the whole natural universe, and present, spiritually and materially, in every portion of it. (Cf. Windelband,
History of Philosophy; Owen, *Skeptics of the Italian Renaissance;* and
Boulting, *Giordano Bruno.*) His teaching that God is Intellect, Wisdom, and Spirit makes his Deity almost identical with Servetus's. It is,
of course, patent that Milton's conception of God is the direct and inevitable result of the interpretation of Christian dogma in the light of
the rationalistic, pantheistic, and monistic metaphysics of the Renaissance.

The study of the sources of Milton's thought is most dangerous
ground; and scholars should rigorously avoid all but rather obvious
conclusions. Denis Saurat (in *Milton, Man and Thinker*) has advanced
the theory that Milton was heavily dependent upon the *Zohar* and the
Kabbalah; and Marjorie Nicholson has attempted to draw a parallel
between Milton's ideas and some of those appearing in More's *Conjectura Cabbalistica.* (Cf. *Phil. Quarterly,* January, 1927.)

Milton knew almost everything of a philosophical and theological
nature which existed during his day; and it would be strange if he had
no acquaintance with theosophy. But to suppose that he drew as much
from this as from the immeasurably more important writings of the
Greek philosophers, the Christian theologians—orthodox and unorthodox—and the great secular metaphysicians of the Renaissance would be
far stranger still. The danger of extending a likeness that may exist in
a detail or two to a whole system is a most insidious one; and this re-
mark is especially in point here because Milton's keenly rationalistic
and common-sense mind was such as to repel almost involuntarily the
hazy and obscure speculations of the neo-Platonists, etc., who transformed all literal interpretation into symbolism and allegory.

But the service of Denis Saurat to Milton scholarship is a real
one. He has shown that the motivation of Eve, after her fall, for offer-

We must realize one fact before we proceed further: Milton differentiates sharply between the pre-
and the post-gospel Trinity. We will later discuss the

---

ing the fruit to her husband is the same in the *Zohar* as in *Paradise
Lost*. And he has also shown that Milton's "retraction" theory derives
from the same source.

When, however, he says, "This central point once fixed, everything
else derives from it," he states far more than the evidence justifies. As
a matter of fact, the rest of the parallel deals for the most part with
ideas that were common to scores of well-known writers. For example,
the idea that God is light is to be found in the Nicene Creed; the conception of the Demiurge was an old Gnostic teaching (the Gnostics, of
course, were closely related to the neo-Platonists); the idea that the
universe is a single substance and is God was the original postulate of
all Renaissance pantheism; the idea that sex is good and legitimate was
denied only by the ascetics; the belief that woman is inferior to man
was never questioned until recently; and the teaching that the female
is a complement to the male is at least as old as Plato. Miss Nicholson
is also careless in this matter: the idea that the reason and the passions are opposed is found in all pagan ethics. The most important
words she italicizes in the passages from More and Milton are to be
found in Genesis 3 : 4–5. This is "the common source."

It is futile to try to draw a parallel between Milton's thinking and
the Gnostic or neo-Platonic teaching concerning emanations—the En-
Sof, the Sephiroth, etc. There is nothing in our poet to justify such a
proceeding. And to say that Satan attacked the feminine aspect of
Adam is to read into Milton an interpretation which no one could have
dreamed of, except to show that he had read the *Kabbalah*. And, in
drawing a parallel between Milton's and More's creative agencies, Miss
Nicholson leaves out of the account all consideration of the Willing and
Energic Aspects of God; for in More nothing is said about them.

The most significant theory to discuss in this connection is that of
matter; and here we find that a vast gulf separates Milton from the
Kabbalists, and the theosophists in general. These thinkers drew their
ideas from the ancient dualistic philosophers, and, consequently, they

Son, or Christ; but here we ought to notice the post-gospel status of the Son and the Holy Ghost. He says:

> Since, therefore, the Son derives his essence from the Father,[11] he is posterior to the Father not merely in rank . . . . but also in essence.

And concerning the Holy Ghost:

> He is a minister of God, and therefore a creature . . . . created or produced . . . . later than the Son, and far inferior to him.

There is here neither equality nor a trinity; but in these quotations Milton is dealing with the post-gospel Son and with the special spirit or Holy Ghost, "promised

---

are much nearer to Augustine in their conception of matter than they are to Milton, who was dependent upon Renaissance pantheism. Without exception, Plotinus, the authors of the *Zohar* and the *Kabbalah*, Robert Fludd, Jacob Boehme, etc., looked upon matter as evil and essentially different from spirit. This metaphysical dualism, which is common also to all orthodox Christian theologians of the Western Church, appears in Henry More as well: Miss Nicholson is mistaken in saying that Milton's teaching is the same as More's in regard to matter and the relation between the soul and the body. More says, "Every man living on the face of the earth hath these two Principles in him, *Heaven* and *Earth, Divinity* and *Animality, Spirit* and *Flesh*" (*Writings of Henry More*, 1662, "Conjectura Cabbalistica," p. 29); and again: "The soul of man . . . . is united to a terrestrial body" (*ibid.*, p. 20).

To point out all the differences between Milton and the Kabbalists or More would be a much more comprehensive undertaking than to summarize those between Milton and Calvin. The fact probably is that Milton borrowed from a thousand different sources; and it is certain that the bulk of what we find in him was widely known during his day. Servetus and Milton, however, have several extraordinary resemblances; and they are in disagreement on *no* significant point.

[11] Milton here, of course, refers to the Son, the *man* Jesus.

alike and given, To all Beleevers." We have nothing to do with these in *Paradise Lost,* or in Milton's general metaphysics.

Before glancing at the passages in Milton's works which express his doctrine of God, it may be well to sum up his general conception.

As a basis for it, we have a monistic pantheism,[12] a single, unified substance in the entire universe which is God himself. In this substance or essence there are not various existences, but three aspects of the same existence, three manifestations of one reality. God the Father is the material of the cosmos, and also will or destiny[13]—the fundamental (perhaps Milton means the psychical and physical) law which governs all spirit, matter, and motion—all relations between cause and effect; God the Word is the energic force in the universe, the power of action, creation, effectual strength—it is God exhibited as power or might; God the Spirit is nothing definite: he is illumination, vitality, irradiance. These three aspects of godhead are found in the

----

[12] I speak here of "monistic pantheism" because the ancient absolute metaphysical dualists—such as Hermogenes—postulated in effect a dualistic pantheism, the two gods existing everywhere in conflict with each other. They were directly under the influence of the Christianized Zoroastrianism which we call by the name of "Manichaeism." As Schopenhauer says ("The Christian System"), the Christian conception of God and the Devil are similar to the Persian Ormuzd and Ahriman.

[13] Cf. *P. L.,* X, 68. In *ibid.,* II, 198, we read,

> "Fate inevitable
> Subdues us, and Omnipotent Decree,
> The Victors will."

cosmos as a whole (where they constitute the Trinity or God) and in every portion of the cosmos—in every rock, stream, tree, animal, man, and angel. In all living things, from the lowliest herb to man, we have substance, energy, and animation. Without these nothing can exist; at least, it cannot exhibit the mysterious life-giving principle. Just as my body, my strength, and my warmth or animation are all myself—and none of these more so than any other—just so are the Father, the Word, and the Spirit all the same thing; they are but differing aspects of God in the universe.

Much in the *Christian Doctrine* tends to establish the sense of the preceding paragraph; but there Milton was the explicit and suspected theologian, who was compelled to be wary, who did little more than suppress, who wished to teach only the doctrines essential to salvation, and who, most important of all, was dealing with post-gospel theology. It was in *Paradise Lost* that Milton was freed from utilitarian aims and the pressure of hostile criticism; there could his imaginative metaphysical conceptions find untrammeled play; and it is chiefly there that we must seek his conception of the Deity.

The relationship existing among the members of the Trinity is made clear in a number of passages, of which the following are important:

Mean while the Son[14]
On his great Expedition now appeer'd.

[14] Here, of course, called the *Son* Platonically.

> And thou, my Word, begotten Son, by thee
> This I perform, speak thou, and be it don.
>
> Father Eternal, thine is to decree
> Mine both in Heav'n and Earth to do thy will.

It is evident that God creates the world, even though, specifically, the *Word* performs the act. The two are as inseparable as the convex and the concave of a curve. But still more important are the following lines, in which the "King of Glorie" (God the Father) is identified with the Word and Spirit—his manifeſtations:

> The King of Glorie in his powerful[15] Word
> And Spirit coming to create new worlds.[16]

It is God, then, who is coming, but in the form of Word and Spirit. It is obvious that the three must be various aspects of the same thing. The Word and Spirit are modes by which the Willing Power communicates itself into sense. Again:

> The Creator from his work
> Desisting, though unwearied, up return'd
> Up to the Heav'n of Heav'ns his high abode
> Thence to behold this new created World
> Th' addition of his Empire, how it shew'd
> In prospect from his Throne, how good, how faire,
> Answering his great Idea.

Analysis of this passage reveals the fact that no differentiation is here made between God the Father and God the Word. The latter is called the Creator; not merely

---

[15] "Powerful" should here be taken to mean "might-possessing."

[16] Cf. also *P. W.*, IV, 170–71.

him *by whom*[17] the things were made. The Empire is
called his, as well as the Throne, and the archetypal
Idea. It must be evident that whatever it was that went
into the Deep, it was not a being separate from the
Father, nor yet the Father himself in his original ca-
pacity, but a manifestation of him. The Word is simply God communicating himself into sense. In heaven
the Word and the Father are represented as speaking
to one another, but God is always invisible and inaudi-
ble.[18] This speaking is the adaptation of God to human
comprehension, which Milton must concede to our human weakness and his own. We find here expressed the
conception of a modal Trinity.

We should notice Milton's expressions concerning
the functions of those aspects of Deity which he calls
by the names of Father and Word. Throughout *Paradise Lost* we necessarily notice that God *does* nothing.
He "utters [metaphorically] his voice" from the midst
of a golden cloud; he is surrounded and hidden by divine effulgence; the archangels are his eyes.[19] When Satan and his followers rebel, Michael, with his warriors,
is first sent against them; next the Word, Platonically
called[20] "Messiah" or the "Son," goes forth to battle.
The Word, too, created the heavens and the earth and

[17] Cf. *P. W.*, IV, 172.   [18] Cf. *ibid.*, p. 109.

[19] *P. L.*, III, 650.

[20] We learn this especially from the following passage of the *Christian Doctrine:* "The Son existed in the beginning, under the name of
Logos or *Word*, and was the first of the whole creation, by whom afterwards all other things were made both in heaven and earth."

all creatures in them; it was he who, assuming the humanized form, became Jesus, the man, who thus performed the will of God; and, lastly, it is he who is now the mediator between God and man. The Father remains always inscrutable and unknowable. He is

> Omnipotent,
> Immutable, Immortal, Infinite,
> Eternal King; thee, Author of all Being,
> Fountain of Light, thy self invisible
> Amidst the glorious brightness where thou sit'st
> Thron'd inaccessible, but when thou shad'st
> The full blaze of thy beams, and through a cloud
> Drawn round about thee like a radiant Shrine,
> Dark with excessive light thy skirts apeer,
> Yet dazle Heav'n, that brightest Seraphim
> Approach not, but with both wings veil thir eyes.

It is otherwise with the Word: it is he who reveals the Father. He is acting, visible, audible; he is God's "Wisdom and effectual might." In him is all the Father "substantially expressed." He is the "divine similitude," "the effulgence of God's glory," etc. "The Word," says Milton, "was audible. But God, as he cannot be seen, so neither can he be heard."

God says:

> My Word, my Wisdom, and effectual might.

> Son, thou in whom my glory I behold
> In full resplendence, Heir of all my might.

> Effulgence of my Glorie, Son belov'd,
> Son in whose face invisible, is beheld,
> Visibly, what by Deitie I am.

> Begotten Son, Divine Similitude,
> In whose conspicuous count'nance without cloud,
> Made visible, the Almightie Father shines.

Other passages treating the same subject express the same idea:

> Beyond compare the Son of God was seen
> Most glorious, in him all his Father shon
> Substantially express'd.

> Thus saying, from his radiant Seat he rose
> Of high collateral glorie.

>   On his right
> The radiant image of his Glory sat
> His onely Son.

> All his Father in him shon.

The fact that the Word is nothing but the visible, audible, and effectual expression of God must be clear. We are further convinced of the identity of the Father and the Word by the following passage, spoken by the Creator to Adam:

> What thinkst thou then of mee, and this my State?
> . . . . who am alone
> From all eternitee, for none I know
> Second to mee or like, equal much less;
> How have I then with whom to hold converse
> Save with the creatures which I made, and those
> To me inferior, infinite descents
> Beneath what other creatures are to thee?

Who is it that speaks this? It cannot be God the Father, because he has never been seen or heard, as Milton asserts. Yet the being is called "the Almighty." Adam also calls this divine presence his "Maker," etc. The speaker must be the Word, the Son, he who brought the world into existence; and he is identified with the Father. We read that God knows no other who is not infinite descents beneath himself. But surely one would not say that he who "substantially expressed" the Father, that he who is the heir of all his might, who is his radiant image, is infinite flights below him; or that he who, being the divine similitude and the effulgence of his glory, makes visible what by Deity God invisibly is, and he in whom all the Father shines, is such. And we find throughout that Milton speaks in this way concerning the Word, and, to a lesser extent, perhaps, of the Spirit. The Word and Spirit are simply God apparent.

Milton's explicit statements concerning the Holy Spirit carry out the conception of modality:

Nor has the word *spirit* any other meaning in the sacred writings, but that breath of life which we inspire, or the vital, or sensitive, or rational faculty, or some action or affection belonging to those faculties.

When the phrase, the Spirit of God, or the Holy Spirit, occurs in the Old Testament,[21] it is to be variously interpreted; sometimes it signifies God the Father himself . . . . sometimes the power and virtue of the Father, and particularly that divine breath or influence by which every thing is created and nourished.[22] Sometimes it means that impulse or voice of God by

[21] Notice that Milton is here careful to refer. to the pre-gospel Trinity only.

[22] The Spirit of God, we see, is the life-giving principle in the world.

which the prophets were inspired. . . . . Undoubtedly neither David nor any other Hebrew, under the Old Covenant, believed in the personality of that *good* and *Holy Spirit.*

Nothing can be more certain than that all these passages [quoted by Milton from the scriptures], and many others of a similar kind in the Old Testament were understood of the virtue and power of the Father. . . . .

From the preceding and the following, as well as from many other passages in Milton, we learn that he conceived of the general spirit of God as being God himself, his mode of vitalizing manifestation:

With regard to the annunciation made to Joseph and Mary, ... the Holy Spirit . . . . is not to be understood with reference to his own person alone. For it is certain that, in the Old Testament, under the name of the Spirit of God, or of the Holy Spirit, either God the Father himself, or his divine power was signified. . . . . "The Spirit of God moved upon the face of the waters"; that is, his divine power, rather than any person. . . . . I am inclined to believe . . . . that it is the Father himself who is here [Matt. 41:31, 32] called the Holy Spirit.[23]

The Holy Spirit, then, is the virtue and power of the Father, a breath, an impulse, or the influence by which everything is created and nourished; he is God's vitalizing force or mode of revelation; he is as identical with God as my mind is with myself. When Milton says

[23] The quotations we have given here refer only to the General Spirit of God, which is a member of the modal Trinity. But Milton frequently mentions the Special Spirit or Holy Ghost, as in the passage quoted above (p. 119), and in the following: "The Spirit signifies the person itself of the Holy Spirit, or its symbol. . . . . Lastly it signifies the donation of the spirit itself, and of its attendant gifts." The Holy Ghost is a specialized portion of the General Spirit.

that God sent his Word and Spirit to create new worlds, he merely tells us that the Deity himself went into the Deep in the forms of energizing and vitalizing power.

In *Paradise Lost* we read:

> But on the watrie calme
> His brooding wings the Spirit of God outspred,
> And vital vertue infus'd, and vital warmth
> Throughout the fluid Mass, but downward purg'd
> The black, tartareous, cold, infernal dregs
> Adverse to life.

Milton's Muse, his Urania, whom he addresses as follows, is simply the General Spirit of God:

> Sing, Heav'nly Muse, that on the secret top
> Of Oreb, or of Sinai, didst inspire
> That Shepherd, who first taught the chosen Seed,
> In the Beginning how the Heav'ns and Earth
> Rose out of Chaos.

and again:

> Before the Heavens thou wert, and at the voice
> Of God, as with a Mantle didst invest
> The rising world of waters dark and deep
> Won from the void and formless infinite.

The Muse is the spirit of God in both its general and special aspects:

> And chiefly Thou, O Spirit, that dost prefer
> Before all Temples th' upright heart and pure,
> Instruct me, for Thou know'st; Thou from the first
> Wast present, and, with mighty wings outspread,
> Dove-like satst brooding on the vast Abyss,
> And mad'st it pregnant; what in me is dark

> Illumine, what is low raise and support;
> That to the highth of this great Argument,
> I may assert Eternal Providence,
> And justifie the wayes of God to men.

In this conception of God, we see Milton's modernity again. It is, first of all, obvious that he had freed himself completely from the tyranny of the orthodox and irrational creed. But far more significant is the fact that his theology is as modern as any can be. It is essentially the theory of Browning, Swinburne, Emerson, Whitman, Samuel Butler, and Edward Carpenter. In fact, it is not far removed from the belief of any vitalist. Few people deny that the principle of life is mysterious, quite beyond scientific analysis; every hypothesis made to explain that mystery must be metaphysical. Milton's theory of God is not only rational but most reasonable; it is an exposition of the universe which we can all accept. And the truth is that most modern thinkers do accept it in whole or in part.

The third great conception in Milton's metaphysical system is his theory of matter. Here it is more obvious that he is diametrically opposed to the orthodox doctrine than in most of his metaphysics. For many centuries the church had insisted that God created the world "out of nothing." But Milton boldly proclaimed that matter and God are identical, that matter is essentially good, that it is eternal, and that "no created thing can be finally annihilated." This pantheism we find expressed again and again:

> Boundless the Deep, because I am who fill
> Infinitude, nor vacuous the space.

God *is* the boundless Deep, the infinite substance which is omnipresent in the cosmos, which, however, is endued with various forms and degrees of perfection: this is Renaissance pantheism:[24]

> One Almighty is, from whom
> All things proceed, and up to him return,
> If not deprav'd from good, created all
> Such to perfection, one first matter all,
> Indu'd with various forms, various degrees
> Of substance, and in things that live, of life.

This boundless "deep," this "first matter" not yet "indu'd with various forms" is the stormy chaos, the

> Wilde Abyss,
> The Womb of Nature and perhaps her Grave,
> Of neither Sea, nor Shore, nor Air, nor Fire,
> But all these in their pregnant causes mixt
> Confus'dly, and which thus must ever fight,
> Unless th' Almighty Maker them ordain
> His dark materials to create more worlds.

In *The Christian Doctrine*, Milton says:

With regard to the original matter of the universe, however, there has been much difference of opinion. Most of the moderns contend that it was formed from nothing, a basis as unsubstantial as that of their own theory.

It is clear then that the world was framed out of matter of some kind or other. For since action and passion are relative terms, and since, consequently, no agent can act externally, unless there be some patient, such as matter, it appears impossible that

[24] Cf. Windelband, *History of Philosophy*, pp. 366–77.

God could have created this world out of nothing; not from any
defect of power on his part, but because it was necessary that
something should have previously existed capable of receiving pas-
sively the exertion of the divine efficacy. Since, therefore, both
Scripture and reason concur in pronouncing that all these things
were made, not out of nothing, but out of matter, it necessarily
follows, that matter must either have always existed independently
of God, or have originated from God at some particular point of
time. That matter should have been always independent of God
. . . . that matter, I say, should have existed of itself from all
eternity, is inconceivable. If on the contrary it did not exist from
all eternity, it is difficult to understand from whence it derives its
origin. There remains, therefore, but one solution of the difficulty,
for which moreover we have the authority of Scripture, namely,
that all things are of God.

Substance [is to be] considered an efflux of Deity. . . . . In
the first place, there are, as is well known to all, four kinds of
causes,—*efficient, material, formal,* and *final.* Inasmuch then as
God is the primary, and absolute, and sole cause of all things, there
can be no doubt but that he comprehends and embraces within
himself all the causes above-mentioned. Therefore the material
cause must be . . . . God. . . . . Matter . . . . proceeded incorrupti-
ble from God. . . . . It is an argument of supreme power and
goodness, that such diversified, multiform and inexhaustible virtue
[as matter] should exist and be substantially inherent in God . . . .
and that this diversified and substantial virtue should not remain
dormant within the Deity, but should be diffused and propagated
and extended as far and in such manner as he himself may will.
For the original matter of which we speak, is not to be looked
upon as an evil or trivial thing, but as intrinsically good. . . . . It
was a substance, and derivable from no other source than from the
fountain of every substance, though at first confused and formless,
being afterwards adorned and digested into order by the hand of
God.

We find, then, that God is identical with the physical universe; that chaos is only that part of God's body[25] which is not yet under law; and that matter, being not only from but also of God, is—as the modern scientist also says—eternal, inannihilable.

This metaphysical conception had vast practical consequences. "The original matter of" the universe "is not . . . . an evil or trivial thing, but . . . . intrinsically good, and the productive stock of every subsequent good." If everything is a portion of God, nothing really evil can exist; there is no room for it in the system of things; it is simply the absence of good—a negative quality like darkness and cold. At a single stroke, the dualism of Augustine, with its fearful sting and the omnipresent pessimism which it induces, vanishes like mist before the sun! The basis for everything that Calvin, Luther, and Puritanism stand for is abolished and obliterated. With Milton's Renaissance metaphysics the doctrines of human depravity, impotence, and need for absolute dependence upon external forces become untenable. To a man who believes that man's body is a portion of God and that his reason is an incarnation of the Deity, Puritan ethics necessarily become monstrous. The metaphysics of Milton constitute a most powerful and far-reaching weapon in the revolt against the Puritan philosophy of life. And it was this revolt, of which Milton was but one powerful champion, that paved the way for modern life.

[25] Bruno called the world a vast animal, alive with the spirit of God.

Milton's teaching concerning creation is the inevitable outcome of his theory of God and matter. "The original matter," he says, ..., though at first confused and formless [was] afterwards adorned and digested into order by the hand of God." When creation occurs, God merely sends his Word, or effectual might, and his Spirit, or vitalizing power, into chaos; they reclaim a portion of the boundless abyss, the realm of anarchy and misrule, and subject it to law, order, reason. Nothing new comes into existence; but a portion of God's passive principle (matter), as yet uninformed either with vitality or law, is filled by the one and constructed by the other into order. Uriel says:

> I saw when at his Word the formless Mass
> This worlds material mould came to a heap:
> Confusion heard his voice, and wilde uproar,
> Stood rul'd, stood vast infinitude confin'd;
> Till at his second bidding darkness fled,
> Light shon, and order from disorder sprung.

When God creates, he merely "puts forth his goodness," as he may choose to do or abstain from doing. Metaphorically, he addresses the second member of the Trinity:

> My Word, my Wisdom, and effectual Might,

who, on his part, uses language such as follows:

> Father Eternal, thine is to decree,
> Mine both in Heav'n and Earth to do thy Will.

The Word goes forth into

> the vast immeasurable Abyss,
> Outrageous as the Sea, dark, wasteful, wilde,
> Up from the bottom turn'd by furious windes
> And surging waves, as Mountains to assault
> Heav'ns highth, and with the Centre mix the Pole.
> Silence, you troubl'd waves, and, thou Deep, peace,
> Said then th' Omnific Word, your discord end.

. . . .

> . . . . Chaos heard his voice.

When the Creator returns (the Father and the Word being evidently the same individual), he sees

> from his prospect high,
> Wherein past, present, future, he beholds,

the new world,

> how good, how faire,
> Answering his great Idea.

Notice this last expression: like the human architect, God had a conception of what was to be constructed before any of the actual labor was performed; and it was this pre-existing idea which God realized in creating. Perhaps for God, the infinite living One, the idea is itself identical with its realization. "Immediate are the acts of God," because his power is infinite and communicates itself into sense by fiat. Nevertheless, we must understand that, in creating, God works according to his power and his means, just as a human engineer, in constructing a bridge, labors according to his.

The fact that matter and spirit are, in Milton's metaphysics, but two aspects of an identical reality is impressed upon us more than once in his writings. The old dualism of Paul, Augustine, Luther,[26] and, indeed, the whole Western Catholic church, as well as all Reformation thinking, has utterly vanished in Milton under the influence of Renaissance philosophy. Milton says

> Man is a living being, intrinsically and properly one and individual, not compound or separable . . . . the whole man is soul, and the soul man, that is to say a body, or substance individual, animated, sensitive, and rational . . . . the breath of life was . . . . an inspiration of some divine virtue.

The idea that matter, the human body, and the visible world itself are in any way inherently evil is utterly repugnant to this new thought. It is true that the mind is superior to the body: but this does not mean that the latter is in any way corrupt; the difference is one, not of kind, but of degree. Mind, spirit, intelligence, are active principles: matter is, we read, "passive." But one is a more and the other only a less elevated manifestation of God himself. Thus it is that the finite creature can, as Plotinus and Bruno taught and as Spenser said in his "Hymne to Heavenlie Beautie," become more and more like the highest essence of Deity by inclining himself toward God—by living in accordance

[26] Luther said: "Man consists of a double nature, spiritual and corporal, and these two are contrary, the spirit fighting the flesh and the flesh the spirit" (Smith's *Martin Luther*, p. 92).

with Reason, the fundamental law of the Universe. Likewise, by trampling Reason under his feet man progressively degrades himself. The fate of the finite creature, then, is in his own hands. He may transform the lowest aspect of his unitary nature into the higher, or he may do the reverse; all depends upon the will, whether the creature shall realize his lowest or highest potentialities. That matter and spirit are, in man as in the whole universe, but a dichotomy, we learn especially from two passages of Milton's poetry: one in *Comus,* the product of youth; the other in *Paradise Lost,* the product of philosophic maturity. We see thus that Milton's theory of matter and spirit remained unchanged throughout his life:

> Till oft convers with heav'nly habitants
> Begin to cast a beam on th' outward shape,
> The unpolluted temple of the mind,
> And turns it by degrees to the souls essence,
> Till all be made immortal: but when lust
> By unchaste looks, loose gestures, and foul talk,
> But most by leud and lavish act of sin,
> Lets in defilement to the inward parts,
> The soul grows clotted by contagion,
> Imbodies, and imbrutes, till she quite loose
> The divine property of her first being.

The idea is repeated in *Paradise Lost:*

> Time may come when Men
> With Angels may participate, and find
> No inconvenient Diet, nor too light fare;
> And from these corporal nutriments perhaps
> Your bodies may at last turn all to Spirit

> Improv'd by tract of time, and wingd ascend
> Ethereal, as wee, or may at choice
> Here or in Heav'nly Paradises dwell.

We need not consider this transformation a mere fancy with Milton: he probably took it very seriously. And, in all sober earnest, is it really unreasonable to believe that man, who has, as science tells us, developed from a little mass of quivering jelly, may, with a lesser further evolution, be able to throw off the dross of his material body and sail upon the depths of azure blue? May not this potentiality be realized in a few ages, in an eon or two?

Milton's doctrine of soul-sleeping, held by other heretics of his time—of whom Richard Overton seems to have been the leader—is the direct and inevitable result of his doctrine concerning spirit and matter. Both being identical with the human individuality, it is impossible that one should exist without the other. Adam, who does not understand the latter elements of the doctrine, but who reasons, as far as he goes, exactly like Milton in the *Christian doctrine,* says:

> Yet one doubt
> Pursues me still—least all I cannot die;
> Least that pure breath of Life, the Spirit of Man
> Which God inspired, cannot together perish
> With this corporeal clod; then, in the Grave,
> Or in some other dismal place, who knows
> But I shall die a living Death? O thought
> Horrid, if true! Yet why? It was but breath

> Of Life that sinn'd; what dies but what had life
> And sin? the Bodie properly hath neither.
> All of me then shall die: let this appease
> The doubt, since humane reach no further knows.

At death, the soul does not,[27] according to the teaching of the church, pass to another sphere to continue consciousness there; but it ceases to have individuality or identity. Until the day of judgment, the human constitution, materially and spiritually, merely resolves itself back into the material and spiritual cosmos, which is God. It is thus that Milton interprets the verse from Ecclesiastes: "Then shall the dust return to the earth as it was; and the spirit shall return to God who gave it." The lapse between death and judgment will be unnoticeable to man—it will be like a profound and dreamless sleep; thousands or millions of years will be reduced to a point. Then, by a sheer miracle God will call together the matter and spirit which before constituted the individual, and he will be given the status in eternity which he earned for himself on earth.[28] It is evident that it is but a single step and a short one from this doctrine to that of the Stoics and of Whitman, which holds that death is but the disintegration of the human individuality, the commingling backward of it into the divine and infinite matter and spirit of the cosmos, and the final loss of personal, conscious identity.

[27] Of course, Milton's doctrine denies entirely the orthodox conception of the soul.

[28] This doctrine is explained in *Paradise Lost*, X, 782 ff.; and *P. W.*, IV, 270–84.

One of the most important metaphysical problems
of ancient or modern times as well as a central doctrine
in Milton is the theory of evil. With Mani, evil was an
uncreated, immutable, eternal principle, *possessing positive powers*. His philosophy naturally results in an absolute dualism and a trenchant pessimism in regard to
all human existence. At the reverse pole, we have the
metaphysical monism which is the universal divinity of
such men as Emerson and Browning; in their thought
everything is not merely potentially good, but absolutely good now, and *all things are equally excellent:*

> The evil is null, is naught, is silence implying sound;
> What was good shall be good, with, for evil, so much
>   good more.

This excessive and almost blind and childish optimism
depends upon the failure to realize that, in the monistic and divine universe, there may be degrees of existence. In the philosophy of Bruno, however, we find a
more logical and profound solution. He taught that, as
God is everything, there can be nothing positively evil
in the universe; everything is good,[29] at least potentially good. Evil is merely a negative quality, the absence
of good; just as darkness is the absence of light, and
cold the absence of heat. These qualities are nothing

[29] A similar doctrine was held by the ancient Greek pantheists and
moralists. Athanasius, for example, who was deeply under their influence, and who was snatching at any argument to refute the Manichees,
said: "By what is not, I mean what is evil" (*Nicene and Post-Nicene
Fathers*, IV, 6). Bruno, however, had philosophical bases for his doctrine and carried it to its ultimate and logical conclusion.

in themselves. This doctrine obviously takes the sting
out of the Augustinian system. Nevertheless, in Renaissance metaphysics, the absence of positive existence
is a fearful thing: it means chaos, destruction. According to Bruno, that is most good which is nearest God in
the scale of things; and that is least good which is farthest away; and between the best and the worst there is
a long, graduated series of steps. The optimism of this
philosophy, displacing, as it did, the dualism of Mani,
was so great that ecstatic dithyrambs of joy reverberate
throughout the writings of the "God-intoxicated" Bruno
and Spinoza. This theory recognizes the evil of the
world and accounts for it; it does not inculcate an implicit or puerile optimism; but, at the same time, it
points the individual a sure avenue of escape from the
thralldom of evil and also a certain means of exalted self-
realization.

A close study of Milton shows that his theory of
evil is that of Bruno. Good and evil are merely the
relative presence or absence of the active aspects of
Deity. When God creates, he "puts forth his goodness," and, by so doing, brings a portion of the universe
now in the lowest possible status of existence to a
higher plane of being. It is brought nearer God in the
scale of things. As we saw in the passage from *Comus*,
"oft converse with heavenly habitants" will at last
transfigure the whole human being into pure spirituality; and foul lust will imbrute his soul so that she will
lose "the divine property of her first being." Man, of

course, must always remain a portion of God, Deity being identical with all existence; however, by striving upward with all his might, he reaches the highest conceivable plane in pure Reason and spirituality; and, by negating his reason, he goes backward into chaos. In the former process, the body—the less elevated aspect of God in us—becomes slowly transformed to spirit; in the latter, the soul becomes "clotted by contagion" and the whole man is soon made solely material, chaotic, lawless, cold, irrational. The divine Word and Spirit are both withdrawn from him.

A passage in *Comus* gives a deep insight into Milton's theory of evil:

> But evil on it self shall back recoyl,
> And mix no more with goodness, when at last
> Gather'd like scum, and settl'd to it self,
> It shall be in Eternal restless change,
> Self-fed and self-consum'd.

This, of course, is an early but accurate description of that chaos which Milton later describes in *Paradise Lost:*

> A dark
> Illimitable Ocean, without bound,
> Without dimension; where length, breadth, and highth,
> And time, and place, are lost; where eldest Night
> And Chaos, Ancestors of Nature, hold
> Eternal anarchie, amidst the noise
> Of endless warrs, and by confusion stand.
> For hot, cold, moist, and dry, four Champions fierce,
> Strive here for Maistrie, and to Battel bring
> Thir embryon Atoms: they around the flag

> Of each his faction, in thir several clanns,
> Light-armed or heavy, sharp, smooth, swift or slow,
> Swarm populous, unnumber'd as the Sands
> Of Barca or Cyrene's torrid soil,
> Levied to side with warring Winds, and poise
> Thir lighter wings. To whom these most adhere
> Hee rules a moment; Chaos Umpire sits,
> And by decision more imbroiles the fray
> By which he Reigns: next him, high Arbiter,
> Chance governs all . . . . this wild Abyss,
> The Womb of nature and perhaps her Grave. . . . .

The condition here described is *evil*, the only real evil that can exist in a pantheistic cosmos; it is at the opposite pole from the highest or most active Deity and all that it implies; it is without warmth, spirit, light, law, order, or beauty: everything is chaotic, discordant, and inharmonious; it is governed by chance and confusion; it is nothing but a raging, furious, and uncontrollable tumult. It is the source or the womb of the world, or Nature, and that which will again swallow it up, when all temporal things shall have run their course.

We should realize that, with Milton, good is almost identical with constructive action. According to Augustine, man could do nothing but evil; but, according to the pantheist, man, being a portion of God, is naturally a producer of good. The frenzied activity of contemporary life is an ultimate though unrecognized result of this principle. This is what lies behind the statement in the *Areopagitica* commending activity and beginning, "I cannot praise a cloistered and fugitive virtue." We notice throughout that Messiah or Christ is the builder, the constructor, the positive force; he performs the will of God: he brought the terrestrial universe into being; and, as the savior of mankind, he builds up a citadel of virtuous and reasoning strength in the hearts and minds of his followers. But Satan's mission is precisely the reverse: it is his aim to destroy whatever the Word brings into being; he represents cosmical negativity incarnate. He highly resolves:

> To do aught good never will be our task,
> But ever to do ill our sole delight,
> As being the contrary of his high will,
> Whom we resist. If then his Providence
> Out of our evil seek to bring forth good,
> Our labour must be to pervert that end,
> And out of good still to find means of evil.

Just how the evil is to be wrought we learn from his conversation with Chaos, the old Anarch, who rules the dominion of Night. The latter's realm has been encroached upon severely: hell and the terrestrial universe have both been formed out of his previous possessions. It is Satan's purpose to destroy the good of God by reducing the World "To her original darkness and your sway (Which is my present journey)." Man, of course, will likewise be reduced.

It is to be noticed here also that evil could come

into the world only by man's own consent.[30] As long
as man remained upright, the Garden was a veritable
paradise, without thorns or weeds, without any disorder, any possible discomfort to man, or any wrack of
elements. Peace and harmony reigned everywhere. But
as soon as man sinned by disobeying his Reason and
by separating himself from God, all was changed. The
animals glared upon one another, preyed upon the
weaker of their kind, and became the foe of man or
timorous in his presence: thus the harmony of nature
was destroyed—universal enmity replaced universal
love. Every manner of destructive growth emanated
from the earth; and man had to produce his food, which
the soil once yielded without despite, by the sweat of
his brow. Storms began to rage, and mankind to feel
the extreme rigors of alternate heat and cold. Discord,
war, and frenzied hate sprang up among the human beings themselves, and even more so within themselves
individually: the war between passion and reason went
on unabated, in which, alas! the former was almost in-
variably victorious. But more than all this, the whole
world now fell an easy prey to the wiles of filthy but
meretricious Sin; and all became devoted to the rav-
enous maw of all-devouring Death, through whom created things pass backward to destruction and chaos.

[30] We learn also that it is not the evil thought but the yielding to
temptation that contaminates the mind:

> "Evil into the mind of God or Man
> May come and go so unapprov'd and leave
> No spot or blame behind."

The fable of Sin and Death in *Paradise Lost* is purely symbolic: the great and powerful Satan could, only
with the extremest difficulty, "wing the desolate Abyss";
but as soon as he was, so contemptibly, successful with
Eve, his children, Sin and Death, drawn by a "powerful sympathy," built an enormous bridge from hell-gate
to the world, on which the whole infernal host could
easily traverse the otherwise perilous deep. This was
made possible solely because of man's sin; otherwise
our world would have been impregnable to Sin and
Death. When Eve fell by the Archfiend's flattering
temptation, his purpose, which, but for Christ's intervention would have been completely realized, was already being accomplished. Symptoms strongly indicative of rapid reduction to chaos soon became visible in
every aspect of terrestrial existence.

Intimately related to the theory of good and evil
which has just been outlined is Milton's doctrine of
evolution and progression. As we have already intimated, there is a graduated scale of existence in the
universe; this is fully explained to Adam by Raphael:

> O Adam, one Almightie is, from whom
> All things proceed, and up to him return,
> If not deprav'd from good, created all
> Such to perfection, one first matter all,
> Indu'd with various forms, various degrees
> Of substance, and in things that live, of life;
> But more refined, more spiritous and pure,
> As neerer to him plac't or neerer tending

Each in thir several active Sphears assignd,
Till body up to spirit work, in bounds
Proportioned to each kind. So from the root
Springs lighter the green stalk, from thence the leaves
More aerie, last the bright consummate floure
Spirits odorous breathes: flours and thir fruit
Mans nourishment, by gradual scale sublim'd,
To vital Spirits aspire, to animal,
To intellectual, give both life and sense,
Fansie and understanding; whence the soule
Reason receives, and reason is her being,
Discursive, or Intuitive; discourse
Is oftest yours, the latter most is ours,
Differing but in degree, of kind the same.
Wonder not then, what God for you saw good
If I refuse not, but convert, as you,
To proper substance.

The following are complementary to the passage just given:

In contemplation of created things,
By steps we may ascend to God.

Therefore what he gives
(Whose praise be ever sung) to man in part
Spiritual, may of purest Spirits be found
No ingrateful food: and food alike those pure
Intelligential substances require
As doth your Rational; and both contain
Within them every lower facultie
Of sense, whereby they hear, see, smell, touch, taste,
Tasting concoct, digest, assimilate,
And corporeal to incorporeal turn.
For know, whatever was created needs
To be sustaind and fed; of Elements

The grosser feeds the purer, earth the sea,
Earth and the Sea feed Air, and Air those Fires
Ethereal, and as lowest first the Moon;
Whence in her visage round those spots, unpurg'd
Vapours not yet into her substance turn'd.
Nor doth the Moon no nourishment exhale
From her moist Continent to higher Orbes.
The Sun that light imparts to all, receives
From all his alimental recompense
In humid exhalations, and at Even
Sups with the Ocean.

Together with collateral implications, Milton here emphasizes the following ideas: first, that all things are created perfect, but may degenerate; second, that in the "one first matter," which underlies all existence and is God, there are various degrees of substance, of which some are relatively but not absolutely better than others; third, that the best are those nearest God in the scale of things, and the worst those farthest away; fourth, that spirit is only matter etherealized; fifth, that there is a continuous progression or movement from form to form, from level to level, in the vast homogeneous substance of the Deity; sixth, that all lower forms feed and are turned into those immediately higher in a continuous evolution, until the grossest element becomes the most exalted godhead; seventh, that we, rational, finite beings, may, like the degrees of substance in nature, "by steps ascend to God"; eighth, that we can do so only by being obedient to him, which, we learn otherwhere, is simply observing the law of

Reason; ninth, that man, a being rational and corporeal, may become an angel, a being intelligential and spiritual; tenth, that every degree of being contains within itself all lower forms and faculties, God thus containing everything and man containing all animal, vegetable, and elemental qualities of being besides his own; eleventh, that all existence is fundamentally homogeneous, differing never in kind but only in degree; and, finally, that the Spirit of God, the vitalizing and cognitive power in the universe, appears in every form of existence, but does so in varying degrees—shall we say of concentration? it is vital, animal, intellectual, and intuitive; the last is very nearly pure Reason, or God in his most exalted form. This metaphysical doctrine is in close affinity with that of Walt Whitman, and gives rise to his principle of universal adhesiveness.

Certain incongruities contravene when this metaphysic, formed under secular and pagan influence, is superinduced upon Christianity and especially upon the doctrine of the immortality of the soul.[31] But we have here Milton's basic belief; if it cannot be wholly reconciled with dogma, it is not his fault. Nevertheless, we find a sufficiently thoroughgoing application of it in his theology; man rises to perfection and Deity by observ-

[31] For example, according to his general metaphysics, man goes, upon death, back to chaos if he has lived irrationally; and he becomes one with the universal spirit of God if he has lived in harmony with law; but according to his theology, he goes necessarily either to heaven or to hell, maintaining his personal consciousness there.

ing the law of universal Reason, that is, by putting himself into complete harmony with God.

One fundamental doctrine remains—that of God's relation to man. Here, too, it seems, Milton drew upon Giordano Bruno. The Italian taught that in the universe there is only God and the "monads," the macrocosm and the microcosm, the infinite One and the many finite realities existing within him, which are all his likenesses. Thus man is finitely what God is infinitely. Man contains within him all the aspects of being to be found in the cosmos; and, in his own way, he has the essential powers and qualities of God.

That this is Milton's doctrine we must deduce partially from the general trend of his whole thought rather than by explicit declaration; but we learn from many passages that man is a self-directive unit, that all existence is homogeneous, and that God and man are of the same essence. But, in the *Christian Doctrine*, we are not without distinct teaching concerning this problem. God, says Milton, is an ens,[32] that is, an autonomous being. "Person . . . . signif[ies] any one individual being . . . . any intelligent *ens* numerically one, whether God, or angel, or man." Thus, every intelligent being is, like God, an *ens*. Man is the monad or the microcosm.[33] If he lives lawlessly, he is reduced to the low-

[32] *P. W.,* IV, 86.

[33] The Stoics, Bruno, Boehme, Browne, and many others taught the doctrine of the microcosm, but with varying metaphysical implications.

est possible status of existence. And, likewise, should the entire universe become chaotic, the cosmos or God would indeed still exist, but in a very debased form; it would be reduced to the worst possible condition.

Milton's conviction that all men are, like Christ, sons of God, is the direct consequence of the doctrine we have just discussed. Satan says in *Paradise Regained*:

> Sons of God both Angels are and Men.

> The Son of God I also am, or was,
> And if I was, I am; relation stands;
> All men are Sons of God.

And, in the *Christian Doctrine,* Milton goes even farther, declaring that the name of God may be applied "even to angels and man," when they represent God or receive a message from him.[34] It is obvious that only a single step intervenes between this conception of man and the androdeism[35] of Whitman and Swinburne, which is the ultra-modern theory of God.

Finally, it is ncessary to dwell, for a moment, on the theory of universal and finite Reason. The Stoics taught that there is a universal Reason in the cosmos, which is providence or God, the law with which all men must live in harmony if they would be free and happy. Bruno, like them, maintained further that the individual reason of man is but a small portion of this world-reason; but he made a concrete and highly practical application of a

[34] *Ibid.,* pp. 107-9.   [35] Apotheosis of man.

metaphysical principle when he declared that to compel the convictions of men is to insult God, the indwelling divine faculty that belongs to all. Thus, religious persecution is the most horrible affront that can possibly be offered to the Deity; and man must have unqualified and untrammeled right to think and to speak as seems right to him.

The evidence indicating this to be Milton's philosophy also is definite and extensive. Reason he calls "the image of God." He says,

The existence of God is further proved by . . . . conscience, or right reason, which even in the worst of characters, is not altogether extinguished. If there were no God, there would be no distinction between right and wrong; the estimate of virtue and vice would entirely depend on the blind opinion of men.

God is that force of Reason in the cosmos, that universal distinction between right and wrong, of which every man receives a portion when he is inspired with the breath of life, or the divine virtue.[36] This is exactly the doctrine of the Stoics, who said that we must respect the divine faculty (the daemon) within the mind. "The Spirit of God," says Milton, "dwelleth in us." "Nor has the word *spirit* any other meaning in the sacred writings but that . . . . rational faculty." Right reason or conscience consists of "those unwritten laws and ideas which nature hath engraven in us." It is "the law of nature . . . . the only law of laws truly and properly to all mankind fundamental." Coercion in religion, says Milton, is an

[36] *Ibid.*, IV, 188.

attempt to compel the spirit of God. By all this, and more of the same nature, it is clear that man's "reason" is "that spiritual illumination which is common to all," and is a finite portion of that aspect of God which is his spirit and which is the basic law of the cosmos. Here again Milton was obviously in revolt against Puritanism and all that it stood for, and startlingly modern in point of view.

We pass now to a consideration of one or two metaphysical doctrines which are distinctly theological.

RELIGIOUS METAPHYSICAL DOCTRINES

The first conception here to be touched upon is the theory of the Incarnation. Milton was essentially a Eutychian, that is, he maintained that Christ's was not a dual but a single nature.[37] He held, furthermore, that Jesus was a man:

> till one greater man
> Restore us.

> So Man, as is most just
> Shall satisfie for Man, be judg'd and die.

He is

> This perfect man, by merit called my Son.

All this follows naturally from his metaphysics. All substance being homogeneous, it is impossible that Christ have, according to the orthodox conception, two distinct natures. God being identical with all substance and also

[37] For a full discussion of this, cf. *P. W.*, IV, 288-95.

an absolute unity,[38] it is impossible that any duality exist in any manifestation of himself. And the same line of reasoning is valid with regard to the humanity of Jesus. He was the son of God, as are we all his sons, being made of his spirit and his substance, and endowed, finitely, with all the same qualities which he possesses infinitely. He was a man, like all of us, being composed of the same nature as ourselves and endowed with a similar rational faculty and corporeal body. In this point, then, Milton is a modern Unitarian.

One further and final point remains—the doctrine of the will. We have quoted, on a previous page, Prynne's dogmas concerning this, which constitute the orthodox conception, based, as we have also pointed out, upon the doctrine of human depravity. But Milton proceeded on different ethical and metaphysical bases, which led to a different theory of volition. He believed that ethical reality exists within the human mind, alone; that evil is merely negative; that man, a likeness of God in the small, is a material and spiritual manifestation of him and must, therefore, be at least potentially good; that it is impossible for virtue to exist without responsibility and power of committing sin at will; and that man's reason is the indwelling spirit of God.

The importance of Milton's revolt in declaring for theological libertarianism can scarcely be overestimated. By this he proclaimed man a more or less autonomous unit, even in theology, the most tyrannous of all human

[38] Cf. *ibid.*, pp. 25–27.

disciplines. With almost ineffable courage he dared to maintain that the authority of the unseen must become less. Theological libertarianism was no mere speculative theory: it was a principle subversive of all that medievalism (or Puritanism) implies; it declared man free, responsible, self-dependent even with respect to his eternal destiny. It meant that the tyranny of the priest was about to disintegrate.

There have been three great aspects in the problem of the will, with one of which almost every great ancient and modern thinker has been concerned. The first is the ethical, and was treated by the pagan moralists, who concluded that man's happiness lies in his own hands. The last is the modern, the psychological, which attempts to establish or disprove the theory that all action and thought are the inevitable result of pre-existing forces. But the theological problem was this: what had God determined in regard to the salvation or damnation of mankind?[39] The crux of the solution lay outside man and was concerned with the purposes of God. The solution itself, however, was freighted with immensely practical implications. Under absolute predestination the only logical philosophy is one of implicit faith in the unknown and the incomprehensible, of self-abnegation and self-distrust, of contempt for human righteousness and reason. It demands a life of passive contemplation, of hatred for human activity or accomplishment. Under

[39] Milton is indebted to Jacobus Arminius for many of his libertarian arguments.

free will the logical philosophy is one of activity, of reason and self-elevation, of love, of virtue and human excellence. The former naturally inculcates slavery of every kind, especially the slavery of the mind; the latter necessarily leads to freedom and self-expression.

This very important teaching finds complete and parallel expression in the *Christian Doctrine* and *Paradise Lost*. The reconciliation of absolute prescience with individual freedom, between which Milton draws a distinct line of demarkation,[40] is one of the greatest problems:

Nothing happens of necessity because God has foreseen it; but he foresees the event of every action because he is acquainted with their natural causes, which, in pursuance of his own decree, are left at liberty to exert their legitimate influence. Consequently, the issue does not depend on God who foresees it, but on him alone who is the object of the foresight. . . . . The prescience of the Deity . . . . is intransitive and has no external influence.

The following is fundamental in all Milton's thought:

Undoubtedly the prescience of the Deity . . . . can neither impose any necessity of itself, nor can it be considered at all as the cause of free actions. If it be so considered, the very name of liberty must be altogether abolished as an unmeaning sound; and that not only in matters of religion, but even in questions of morality and indifferent things.

Thus he continues the argument:

Since then the apostacy of the first man was not decreed, but only foreknown by the infinite wisdom of God, it follows that pre-

[40] Just as does Erasmus, and also Boethius in his *Consolation of Philosophy*.

destination was not an absolute decree before the fall of man; and
even after his fall, it ought always to be considered as arising, not
so much from a decree itself, as from the immutable conditions of
a decree.

But,

if those decrees of God . . . . were to be understood in an absolute sense without the implied conditions, God would contradict
himself,

and this he cannot do.[41] Milton concludes, therefore, that
"the tenor of the decree as promulged . . . . is uniformly conditional."

Milton turns next to a consideration of what man is
and what power he possesses. "There are," he says,
"some remnants of the divine image left in man."

God has predestinated to salvation, on the proviso of a general
condition, all who enjoy freedom of the will; while none are predestinated to destruction except through their own fault. . . . .
If then God reject none but the disobedient and unbelieving he
undoubtedly gives grace to all, if not in equal measure, at least
sufficient for attaining knowledge of the truth about final salvation. . . . .

God has predestinated from eternity all those who should believe and continue in the faith; it follows that none can be reprobated, except they do not believe or continue in the faith, and even
this rather as a consequence than a decree; there can therefore be
no reprobation of individuals from all eternity.

Thus much, therefore, may be considered as a certain and
irrefragable truth—that God excludes no one from the pale of repentence and eternal salvation.

The following is very important, as an indication,

[41] *Ibid.*, p. 26.

first, of Milton's whole philosophy; and, second, of the arguments which it was necessary for him to confute:

Nor does this reasoning represent God as depending upon the human will, but as fulfilling his own pleasure, whereby he has chosen that man should always use his own will with a regard to the love and worship of the Deity, and consequently with a regard for salvation. If this use of the will be not admitted, whatever worship or love we render to God is entirely vain and of no value; the acceptableness of duties done under the law of necessity is diminished, or rather annihilated altogether, inasmuch as freedom can no longer be attributed to that will over which some fixed decree is inevitably suspended.

The objections, therefore, which some urge so vehemently against this doctrine, are of no force whatever;—namely, that the repentence and faith of the predestinated having been foreseen, predestination becomes posterior in point of time to works,—that it is rendered dependent on the will of man,—that God is defrauded of part of the glory of our salvation,—that man is puffed up with pride,—that the foundations of all Christian consolation in life and in death are shaken,—that gratuitous justification is denied. On the contrary . . . . the glory . . . . of the divine wisdom and justice, is thus displayed.

This theory of the will is harmonious with Milton's theological doctrine concerning Christ's atonement. Quite contrary to the Puritans, he maintained that "Christ . . . . has made satisfaction for all." This general satisfaction naturally gives to all "the power of volition, that is, of acting freely, in consequence of recovering the liberty of the will by the renewing of the Spirit." God's grace, says Milton, "can only imply that he works in us the power of acting freely." Through renovation, man "is raised to a far more excellent state of grace and glory than that from which he had fallen."

Thus we see in the *Christian Doctrine* as in *Paradise Lost* that God has indeed brought good out of evil for man. We feel at the end of the epic that perhaps man is the gainer by the Fall; he has gained knowledge, experience, greater responsibility, the potentiality of experiencing the delight resulting from self-elevation, and the power of appreciating a happiness which he must necessarily contrast with a previous misery. And, as Milton explicitly tells us, the state of those who live in harmony with God is better than that of Adam and Eve in the Garden.[42] This is indeed an optimistic conviction concerning the great Fall!

The same theological doctrines concerning volition are no less central in *Paradise Lost,* and are repeated again and again; it is the way of God to men to give them control over their own eternal fate:

> I formed them free, and free they must remain
> Till they enthrall themselves: I else must change
> Thir nature, and revoke the high Decree
> Unchangeable, Eternal, which ordain'd
> Thir freedom.

Notice that the decree ordaining man's freedom is unchangeable and eternal. Thus God leaves man's

> happie State secure,
> Secure from outward force: within himself
> The danger lies, yet lies within his power;

[42] "A paradise within thee, happier farr."

Against his will he can receive no harme.
But God left free the Will; for what obeyes
Reason, is free, and Reason he made right,
But bid her well be ware, and still erect,
Least, by some faire appeering good surpris'd,
She dictate false, and missinforme the Will.

This, briefly, is Milton's metaphysical system. After we strip his speculations of all their theological encumbrances and the terminology in which they are so frequently involved, this is essentially what remains. We have here a conception of man and the universe which is certainly rational enough; it can indeed in no sense be called scientific—dealing, as it does, for the most part, with problems which are as wholly beyond and above empirical research as is the construction of bridges and skyskrapers outside the scope of metaphysics. Yet many may well say that Milton has given us what is worth more than material wealth or scientific knowledge; he has given us an explanation of life in which all contradiction is solved and in which the mind finds philosophical repose: and this exposition is at least as incapable of disproof as of proof. Nay, it is grounded both upon the eternal verities and upon experience with life, with nature—with all sentient objects. Milton's conceptions, which, by reason of their truth and profoundity, are contemporary with all time, are imbedded in and constitute the background of a sublime cosmical poem, which we cannot comprehend without being thrilled and stricken with awe. I would say, finally, that his whole system of metaphysics is such as may indeed be displaced but can never be superseded; that it constitutes a real and permanent contribution to artistic expression; and that to grasp it thoroughly is, for every man or woman, now and always, to realize a profound joy and a transcendent, boundless satisfaction.

CHAPTER IV

THE EVOLUTION OF MILTON'S THOUGHT

So far as I am aware, no previous author has recognized the fact of change and development in Milton's thought. It seems to have been taken for granted that his ideas with regard to religion, ethics, politics, etc., were definitive when he treated them for the first time. It is true that in regard to divorce, polygamy, toleration, and, in so far as we know, his early metaphysics there was no important change; but in almost every other aspect of his thought there was a distinct evolution.

The failure to understand the broad principles upon which this development is based has led to various rather strange and ludicrous misinterpretations. Even the acute and thoroughgoing Masson supposed that because, in his early pamphlets, Milton condemned Arminius and addressed a sublime apostrophe to the "tripersonal godhead," he was, in youth, orthodox in religion. But this is a most shallow and unphilosophical conclusion. However, one of the most curious misinterpretations of Milton in existence is a lengthy treatise by the Rev. A. D. Barber,[1] who maintains with a mountain of specious evidence that the *Christian Doctrine* was completed by 1641; that ever after that year Milton was a sublapsarian; and that *Paradise Lost* maintains the theory of ab-

[1] *Bibliotheca Sacra* (1859).

solute predestination.[2] The Rev. Barber could not see
that *Paradise Lost* is congruent with the *Christian Doc-trine* in regard to volition; he did not realize that Milton
was, in 1641, without the theological knowledge evi-denced in the *Christian Doctrine;* he is certain that this
work must have been written earlier than any of the
tracts, because Milton is, in these, evidently orthodox
on the point of predestination. He thinks that Milton
gave up a complex and fully elaborated system of heret-ical doctrines—for no assignable reason—and accepted
the current and vulgar opinions within the lapse of a
year. Of course, the thesis is absurd on the face of
things, but it illustrates the possible vagaries to which a
critic, approaching Milton without a broad knowledge
of his intellectual development, is liable.

Nothing occurs without cause; and it is certain that
the change in Milton's attitude and interest, and the evo-lution of his ethical and religious thought were the re-sult of profound experiences. In the present chapter, it
is our purpose, first, to call attention to the changes them-selves; and, second, to explain the reasons for them.

The evolution of Milton's thought was, first, one of
progression toward greater seriousness and profundity;

[2] The article we are referring to is one of many on Milton illus-trating the legalistic and dogmatic attitude. Many, especially clergy-men, have tried to make Milton one of their own party, which Rev.
Barber did, or they have condemned him for not belonging to it. Rev.
Barber says that Augustine, Calvin, and Edwards were those who
taught the "truth" in regard to predestination.

and, second, a movement away from almost pure Renaissance Hellenism (if we can conceive of such a thing) toward the highest ideals and philosophy which Christianity is capable of exhibiting. During the course of the whole change, we find that Milton is attaining a more and more profound conception of human problems, and also that he is becoming less stridently self-dependent. The development of Milton's thought indicates a highly qualified movement toward self-abnegation and surrender to the unseen.

To indicate the change in Milton's thought it will be best, first, to discuss briefly the change in his general interests. We find that these interests before 1655 are overwhelmingly one-world; and that after this date they are eminently—not wholly—two-world. It matters little in what regard we view Milton, we find this generalization holding good.

The change in Milton's occupation serves to establish the proposition. Before 1655 he was variously employed, but never in the interests of the next world or of religion per se. He spent seven years at Cambridge, afterward expressing himself with great contempt concerning the barren theological disputes and sophistries with which the lives of frivolous students were filled.[3] Upon leaving the university, he refused to take holy orders, because his conscience would not permit it.[4] Then, dur-

[3] Cf. *P. W.*, III, 35–39; *ibid.*, pp. 114–15. The same attitude is expressed in other passages.

[4] *Ibid.*, II, 482.

ing five years at Horton, he entered upon a long period of peaceful and extensive study. But this time was in no sense given to religious contemplation; it was a most serious preparation for that sort of gladiatorial intellectual combat which was about to ensue and which Milton entered at the earliest opportunity. We learn from the "Ad Patrem," as well as from numerous other sources, that he desired to dedicate his life to the Muses;[5] and in this desire there was no tinge of theological or even religious impulse. If there was any field in which he was, during the early pamphleteering period, less well versed than we might have expected, it was in theology itself; for we find that many of his early expressions in regard to it are not only very inexact but also quite contrary to his ethical principles. The truth is that Milton was studying ecclesiastical and secular history, literature, music, mathematics,[6] all branches of philosophy, and what was known of science during his day. This is attested, first, by his *Commonplace Book*, in which he took down quotations from his reading; and, second, by the multifarious display of varied learning that we find both in his prose and in his later poetry. Like Bacon, he took all knowledge for his province. In 1638 he began his tour of the Continent, a purely cultural journey, in the course of which he was thrilled by his experiences in

[5] Cf. *ibid.*, I, 254. We find many similar expressions in his early poems and letters. We even find a love for conviviality; cf. especially the "Song on May Morning," and "The Sonnet to the Nightingale."

[6] Cf. *ibid.*, p. 255.

Italy, which gave added impetus to his artistic ambitions. As soon as the great prelatical controversy raged forth in 1641, Milton advanced to the attack; but there was nothing religious in this. He hated the bishops on political, economic, and ethical grounds; he charged them with tyranny, avarice, and corruption; about their theology he said nothing, never even mentioning Laud's Arminianism, with which, in truth, his own ethics were in secret accord. He was the foe to episcopacy because episcopacy was a foe to political freedom and intellectual and artistic expression—not because it misled men in regard to the next world. As soon as the prelates were ousted, Milton turned his attention in other directions. He stepped hastily into an inconsiderate marriage; and the experience growing out of this precipitated *The Doctrine and Discipline of Divorce,* one of the most non-religious, amazing, and modern documents of the seventeenth century. Not long after, in 1644, a law providing censorship for the press provoked the *Areopagitica;* the demand for universal freedom of individual conviction and expression, which is its essence, is as thoroughly one-world as anything can be. After writing a tractate in which he favors pagan education, Milton turned to a scientific investigation of English history; he wrote a heavily documented work running to 1066, in which he exhibited a really modern judgment and use of source-material. There was surely nothing religious in this labor! When, in 1648, Charles I faced a tribunal charging him with high crimes and misdemeanors, and when the Pres-

byterian party *en-masse* were facing about and beginning to defend the King, Milton felt the call to public
duty again, and wrote the *Tenure of Kings and Magistrates,* a purely political document containing the most
modern theories. This made Milton a man of promi-
nence, and he was employed, under the title of Latin Sec-
retary, as the spokesman for the Commonwealth against
its foes at home and abroad. He replied to the *Eikon
Basiliké,* purporting to be written by Charles in prison,
but really composed by a sycophantic bishop, John Gauden;[7] and he confuted Salmasius and Morus. In the
course of these controversies he became blind, losing his
sight, as he later averred with pride and dignity,

> overplied
> In Liberty's defence, my noble task,
> Of which all Europe rings from side to side.

In all the activity which we have just reviewed and
which occupied not less than thirty years, we find a one-
world interest only, to the complete practical exclusion
of all serious thought concerning a future state. Belief,
as Milton somewhere says, is action; a man whose vital
interest is in things of the here and now certainly does
not realize any strong conviction concerning heaven and
hell, although he may have a vague theory concerning
them, based on vulgarly accepted opinion.

After 1655, however, we find a marked change in
Milton's fundamental interest. His three major poems
all deal with the problem of man's relation to God, and

[7] As was discovered much later. Cf. Masson's *Life of Milton.*

do so largely from the religious point of view. Instead of continuing his investigation of English history, he wrote an extensive work on theology, treating the whole field with thoroughness and acumen, and showing a minute knowledge of all dogmatic doctrine and the works of the great theologians. The production of the *De Doctrina Christiana* must have been an enormous labor, especially for a blind man; and nothing could better attest his real interest in the next world than the extraordinary effort he put forth to formulate in every detail and to support by unimpeachable authority and argument the Christian doctrines which he considered essential to salvation. Nevertheless, in spite of the dominating two-world occupation and interest of his later years, he performed a few tasks of a different nature; such were his *Ready and Easy Way to Establish a Free Commonwealth;* his *Treatise of Civil Power in Ecclesiastical Causes, Shewing that it is not Lawful for Any Power on Earth to Compel in Matters of Religion;* his *Considerations Touching the Likeliest Means to Remove Hirelings Out of the Church;*[8] and his final pamphlet demanding religious toleration for all the sects, called *Of True Religion, Heresy, Schism, Toleration.* In the early pamphlets, Milton's references to scripture and theological doctrines and authorities are often rather general and

[8] In this tract Milton maintains that ministers should receive no regular pay at all, or at least only voluntary contributions from their flock, and that they should have some useful trade by which to be self-supporting.

even vague; but we may notice in the later ones that his citations are both more numerous and more exact. The fact is that before 1655 Milton had been totally untouched by those interests which are essentially Puritan and that, after that time, he assumed those interests, at least to a considerable degree.

We must not think, however, that Milton ever became one of the Puritans wholly; he never assimilated more than a portion of their point of view. In his last pamphlet, *Of True Religion,* he defends the so-called errors of the Lutherans, Calvinists, Baptists, Socinians, and Arminians: consubstantiation, supralapsarianism, the denial of paedobaptism, the Trinity, and irresistible grace are all venial faults,[9] for basis can be found for them in scripture and those who hold them are sincere in their opinions. We must insist on nothing not "absolutely necessary to salvation"; and "the hottest disputes among protestants, calmly and charitably inquired into, will be found less than such." To Milton, all Protestant sects seemed to possess equally correct doctrine. The reason was, of course, that he was far less vitally interested in creed and faith than they, and much more engrossed by the ideal of moral perfection and temporal happiness. That is, he had much more of the rational, the ethical, the pagan, the modern, the one-world point of view than they. To the Lutheran the doctrine of the Eucharist was a question of life and death; to Milton,

[9] It is interesting to notice Milton's objective attitude in this pamphlet; for we know that he was himself guilty of some but not of all the "faults" he was defending.

even in maturity, it was almost a matter of indifference.[10] To the Calvinist, belief in supralapsarianism was essential to salvation; but Milton proclaimed free will. The modern rationalist has gone far beyond Milton in attitude toward religion, but in precisely the same direction; he looks upon all religions impartially; and Thomas Paine proposed to construct a rationalistic and philosophic world-religion composed of the best elements to be drawn from Christianity, Mohammedanism, Buddhism, Confucianism, and pagan philosophy.[11] And during the present century a similar proposition has been made by a profound thinker and scholar.[12]

So far we have discussed only the external change; it remains to give an exposition of the internal evolution lying behind it.

There is a distinct change between the characteristics of Milton's early poetic themes and those of his later ones. We may say, first, that the minor poems contain no evidence to show that their author had, as yet, any realization of the great problems of human life. Everything is treated playfully, or at least theoretically; compared with the later poems, they are trivial in content; the only real mastery they achieve is one over language as a poetic instrument. The Italian sonnets deal with fancied emotions; the Latin elegies are, for the most part, little more than artificial and academic exercises.

---

[10] For his discussion of the sacraments, cf. *P. W.*, IV, 413–23.

[11] Cf. *The Age of Reason*.

[12] Cf. E. Carpenter, *Pagan and Christian Creeds*.

They are redolent of the author's classic studies, still fresh in his memory, with which his mind overflows in boisterous ornament. Nowhere do we find any real convictions presented; how could Milton, with his paucity of personal experience, have achieved them? "L'Allegro" and "Il Penseroso," those magical triumphs in exquisite "justness" of language, are without vital thought-content; they are beautiful creations of an idle hour, produced by an ultimate master not yet brought face to face with the grim and stern realities of life. And it is essentially likewise with *Comus*, impeccable creation as it is; the ideal there presented grew not from experience but from the ecstasies resulting from the reading of Spenser and the study of pagan philosophy. It is true that its principles might be applied with far-reaching practical consequences and that later they *were* so applied; but the power of virtue celebrated in the masque is one innocent of all contact with the world—it is theoretical, a force that has never encountered a foe. It is in "Lycidas" that we find the serious note struck for the first time in Milton's poetry, but even this is a personal apotheosis of art and truth and a personal denunciation of greed and corruption rather than an attempt to solve any human problem. Not until he wrote the "Epitaphiam Damónis," lamenting the loss of perhaps the only close friend he ever had, did Milton strike a deeper key. But the symphonic music of "Lycidas" is not present in the Latin hexameters; and the poem on the death of Deodati has not enriched the treasury of our verse.

Nor do any of Milton's early poems embody a religious appeal. The "Ode on the Morning of Christ's Nativity" might be expected to contain such a quality, but it is absent. Christ is simply a great and magnificent king, driving before him the powers of evil and the usurping gods; he is the eradicator of superstition, the bringer of light. Nothing could more accurately indicate Milton's general misapprehension of orthodox Christianity than this poem. That he had no conception of original sin, the depravity of man, the necessity of surrender and self-abnegation is obvious in such poems as "On Time" and "Upon the Circumcision." In "The Passion" we find exemplified Milton's utter inability to think himself into that state of mind which is the essence of Christianity. And *Comus* is diametrically opposed to Puritanism, the utter contradiction of all that it stands for: it is the apotheosis of human virtue and the celebration of its triumphs. Puritanism denies the possible existence of such virtue and demands that man throw himself upon the mercy of the unseen. In neither his Latin nor his English elegy is Milton concerned with the future life; he laments the loss sustained in this one. And we find, too, that his early conception of Deity is far more pagan than Christian. In "Upon the Circumcision," he calls what must stand for God "Justice"; in "Lycidas," he weaves together materials from three or four religions, and Jove seems to be the chief ruler, as is also the case in *Comus*. And we may say, finally, that all of Milton's early poetry is filled not only with pagan myth and imagery but also with pagan thinking; it indicates in no way any real knowledge of Christianity; and it proves beyond doubt that Milton was untouched by the Puritan philosophy during his youth.

Twenty-five years intervened between *Comus* and *Paradise Lost,* and during that time great and various forces were at work. We may say that *Paradise Lost* is half pagan and half Christian: it presents a commingling of two great attitudes toward life; or, we may say it is a treatment of a Puritan theme from a Hellenic point of view. The amalgamation, however, is so complete that the result—something unique in literature—is a perfect artistic unit. In this respect the *Faerie Queene* exhibits a strong contrast; there also the pagan and Christian elements exist in profusion; but they do not mingle: incongruously, they stand side by side. There is an enormous wealth of mythological allusion in *Paradise Lost;* and, even though the poet is often at pains to declare its falsity, there can be no doubt that he revels in its sensuous beauty and half weeps that "the parting genius is with sighing sent." The form of the poem is based upon the pagan epics; the ethics of it are largely Aristotelian; its metaphysic is Renaissance pantheism; its exalted message concerning the ways of God to men is at least as much philosophical—beyond the pale of any religion or period of history—as it is within the limits of Christian dogma. It is true that almost all the chief elements of the whole Christian creed are woven into the fabric in one way or another; but all this is but the framework, the terminology, in the guise of which the poet propounds a broad and profound philosophy of life. And yet we must not minimize the Christian element; it is active throughout. Without a two-world interest to inspire him, Milton would never have composed *Paradise Lost*. He is concerned with the fall of the angels and of man, with the origin and the nature of evil in the universe, with the relation between the infinite and the created, and with the final destiny of man. Had not that for which Christianity chiefly exists been more or less vital to Milton, he could never have been fired to pour the greatest effort of his life into a work of this kind. He accepted the Bible without reservation; but he carried so much into its central teachings that these are wholly transfigured and become totally unlike any other work ever inspired by Christianity.

In *Paradise Regained* we find the evolution carried further. The tone of the whole poem is more somber, and it is less daring both in conception and in execution. Very little mythological allusion or pagan imagery remains. The interest is far more in theology than in metaphysics. All pagan learning and philosophy are condemned, even when the argument is drawn from such sources. The attention is centered upon human temptation and the purpose of Christ in the world. The poem is inferior to *Paradise Lost* in conception because it portrays no real struggle; Satan is simply contemptible, and Jesus is impregnable. We leave the poem as we find it; there is no change in it, only a realization on the part of the duelists of their respective strength and weakness. The whole poem deals with man's power to repel temptation; and this is chiefly a theological problem.

Yet the pagan influence is by no means absent. Had Milton been a Puritan, Christ's victory would have consisted in his death on the Cross, by means of which he took upon himself the burden of man's sins; but now he found it in an intellectual victory which was of a twofold nature: first, a triumph over his own passions; second, a complete refutation of the Adversary's every argument. Milton's is not the suffering but the victorious Christ. Thus he makes his religion one of reason, self-reliance, and personal victory far more than one of surrender and defeat. Even though he was only a semi-Pelagian or a synergist[13] in doctrine, he was almost a Pelagian in practice.[14] For Milton's Christ is rather an examplar of human virtue than one who, by his death, redeems the saints of God.

The completion of the evolution we are treating is reached in *Samson Agonistes*. Here the purely Christian attitude is nearly achieved. There is no ornament, no mythological allusion. Metaphysics form no part of the conception, and no rationalistic theory or doctrine is advanced. All is doubt and uncertainty as to what man ought to do. The only consolation Milton here can find is to throw himself blindly upon the mercy of God and

[13] That is, one who says that the process of salvation is partly carried on by man and partly by God.

[14] That is, one who believes that man both begins and ends the process of his own redemption, Christ being only an excellent exemplar.

trust to the wisdom of his ways, which are beyond our comprehension:

> All is best, though we oft doubt
> What the unsearchable dispose
> Of highest wisdom brings about
> And ever found best in the close.

This is essentially the attitude of surrender which is characteristic of all Puritan thought.

Samson is the epitome of human futility. Ordained by God from birth to a great work, endowed with divine strength, and having lived chastely in every respect, he is yet overcome by temptation—like Adam, with female guile—and he experiences the rigors of punishment and misery. And yet he had never sinned intentionally, and his crime was surely a slight one. On every hand we find people of loose lives and crooked natures who flourish ostentatiously; does God pay no attention either to virtue or to vice? Milton no longer feels able to explain the ways of God; they are inexplicable. Human excellence counts for little or nothing; when everything seems to be going best, one may be on the verge of disaster; and when fortune seems to have carried its victim to its nadir, perhaps he is about to achieve magnificent victory. But everything occurs through an all-wise but inscrutable counsel. Such is the message of *Samson Agonistes*. Man is left almost destitute of power and credit alike; and all glory is given to God.

More curious but no less distinctive is the evolution of Milton's attitude toward women. In youth he was surprisingly ignorant concerning them, and he regarded them as beautiful and fluttering angels clad in exquisite decoration.[15] He seems not to have been aware that they have either physical or moral nature. Until his marriage he seems to have had no real contact with the other sex; and, as we would expect, he knew nothing essential about it.

In 1643, however, he took unto himself a wife. That he married as he did is proof sufficient to establish his ignorance about women; that anything but misery should have resulted from this marriage was impossible. Out of the wreck of his first domestic undertaking, he proceeded to develop a new and twofold ideal: first, a new ideal of woman; second, a new ideal of the marital relationship. In this relationship he regards man as the natural head, and he discusses the whole problem from his point of view. Nevertheless, he accords woman a far higher place than did his contemporaries. He considered her man's intellectual companion, able at all times to carry on "a meet and happy conversation with him." Of course, he regarded woman as created for ends differing from those of man, but both seemed to him equally excellent. In the divorce tracts (1643) and in the two sonnets written to women about the same time,[16] Milton pays them a far higher tribute than would have been possible before his marriage.

In *Paradise Lost* Milton's ideal of woman and the

[15] Cf. the "Elegia Septima" and the Italian sonnets.
[16] Those to Margaret Ley and "To a Virtuous Young Lady."

marital relationship is given poetic expression. The picture of Eve in the Garden is Milton's ideal, not, perhaps, precisely that of the modern feminist!

> When I approach
> Her loveliness, so absolute she seems[17]
> And in her self compleat, so well to know
> Her own, that what she will to do or say
> Seems wisest, vertuousest, discreetest, best.
> All higher knowledge in her presence falls
> Degraded; Wisdom in discourse with her
> Looses, discount' nanc't, and like folly shewes;
> Authoritie and Reason on her waite,
> As one intended first, not after made
> Occasionally; and, to consummate all,
> Greatness of mind and nobleness thir seat,
> Build in her loveliest, and create an awe
> About her, as a guard Angelic plac't.

Yet Milton never forgot that woman is inferior to man in power. On her has been bestowed

> Too much of Ornament, in outward shew
> Elaborate, of inward less exact.
> For well I understand in the prime end
> Of Nature her th' inferiour, in the mind
> And inward Faculties, which most excell.

Eve finds her greatest joy in the admiration of her husband and in her submission to him. He is the god of her life, the source of her strength, and the object of her sole affection. When Adam threw her off with scorn after the Fall, she withered like the stalk severed from its source

---

[17] Notice the unkind "seems."

of nourishment. Eve is indeed the queen of their bower, but Adam is the lord of her.

> Not equal, as their sex not equal seemd;
> For contemplation hee and valour formd,
> For softness shee and sweet attractive Grace,
> Hee for God only, shee for God in him.

Such throughout is the tenor of *Paradise Lost*. To Adam, Eve was in

subjection, but requir'd with gentle sway, ... by her yeilded . . . . with coy submission, modest pride, And sweet reluctant amorous delay.

Such is Milton's ideal of woman and of the marital relationship.

It seems that in later life Milton became less amiable in attitude toward women and more distrustful of them. In *Paradise Lost* he seems to take a kind of pleasure in humbling Eve before her husband; he makes her play a peculiarly ignominious part in the Fall—one more so than the Bible story would require. He portrays the deceits of Dalila, her repulse by Samson, and her unmasking with evident delight. In *Paradise Regained,* Milton makes Satan express scorn for Asmodai's opinion that Christ could be seduced by women and praises Alexander and Scipio, who could be superior to their charms.

> For Beauty stands
> In the admiration only of weak minds
> Led captive; cease to admire, and all her Plumes
> Fall flat.

And in *Samson Agonistes* Milton—anticipating Rousseau, Schopenhauer, and Nietzsche—expresses himself as decisively as follows:

> What e're it be, to wisest men and best,
> Seeming at first all heavenly under virgin veil,
> Soft, modest, meek, demure,
> Once join'd, the contrary she proves—a thorn
> Intestin, far within defensive arms
> A cleaving mischief, in his way to vertue
> Adverse and turbulent; or by her charms
> Draws him awry, enslav'd
> With dotage, and his sense deprav'd
> To folly and shameful deeds which ruin ends.
> What Pilot so expert but needs must wreck,
> Embarqu'd with such a Stears-mate at the Helm?
>
> .   .   .   .
>
> Therefore Gods universal Law
> Gave to the man despotic power
> Over his female in due awe,
> Nor from that right to part an hour,
> Smile she or loure:
> So shall he least confusion draw
> On his whole life, not sway'd
> By female usurpation, nor dismayed.

Thus we see that Milton's attitude toward women underwent a complete change during the course of his experience: first, it was childish admiration for their • mere outside; second, it was high honor, based on heavy • requirements exacted from them; and, third, after many • years of varied experience, it was a final distrust which • bordered on hatred. We must, however, consider this at least partially mere general theory; for we know that he loved his second, and found satisfaction in his third wife, despite the bitterness he felt toward the first one.

There was also a distinct change in Milton's political theory. In the *Areopagitica,* he condemns any law which assumes the common people to be "an untaught and . . . . gadding rout." He is there sure that all are worthy of responsibility and privileges and are able to judge between right and wrong. In the *Tenure of Kings,* written about four years later, we find an attitude that is perhaps even more emphatic; we would expect this in a treatise demanding and justifying[18] the legal execution of an English king—perhaps the most sublime act of courage in the history of the British nation—for the person of Charles was considered almost divine. The political theory here presented is so important that, in another place, we quote from it somewhat at length; it is obvious that the Constitution of the United States is the outgrowth of such thinking as it contains.

"All men," says Milton, "are naturally born free." Throughout he insists on the moral law or right reason of man, which is imbedded in his very nature and by means of which he is naturally superior to all external restraint. The democracy of the *Tenure of Kings and Magistrates* is almost as thoroughgoing as the "liberté, egalité, and fraternité" of the French Revolution.

[18] *The Tenure* was written before the execution and thus demanded it; but it was published after it, for the purpose of justifying it.

But in the *Ready and Easy Way* everything is different; ten years of poignant experience in the midst of stormy and discordant times had served to teach Milton much. In 1659 he is filled with scorn to find that "the inconsiderable multitude are now so mad upon" having a king again.

Nevertheless, Milton hated the monarchical form of government as much as ever; he did not wish to be governed by

a single person, who, for anything wherein the public really needs him, will have little else to do but to bestow the eating and drinking of excessive dainties, to set a pompous face upon the superficial actings of state, to pageant himself up and down in progress among the perpetual bowings and cringings of an abject people, on either side deifying and adoring him for nothing done that can deserve it. For what can he more than another man . . . .?

How unmanly must it needs be to count such a one the breath of our nostrils, to hang all our felicity on him, all our safety, our well-being; for which, if we were aught else but sluggards or babies, we need depend on none but God and our own councils, our own active virtue and industry!

Contrast this with the cringing attitude of Dryden's *Absalom and Achitophel* or his *Hind and the Panther!* How vast the gulf between the ideals and the characters of these famous contemporaries!

Milton's ideal, like Plato's, is "a free commonwealth, wherein they who are the greatest are perpetual servants . . . . to the public at their own cost and charges." The government ought to be entrusted to a "general council of ablest men," which should be perpetual. This should not be a popular assembly, but should consist only of men of distinction. It is evident that in the pamphlet we are discussing, Milton's fear of the mob was as great as his fear of regal tyranny. The people had, by means of a "licentious and unbridled democracy . . . . ruined themselves with their own excessive power." No such thing as universal suffrage, then, ought to exist. Milton says that it will be well to

qualify and refine elections: not committing all to the noise and shouting of a rude multitude, but permitting only those of them who are rightly qualified, to nominate as many as they will.

But it is in *Paradise Regained* that Milton's regard for the common people, once so enthusiastic and later so distrustful, becomes postively scornful. The English had obtained their political desires: they had a debauched degenerate for their king, and him they adored. They had yielded themselves up to "the two most prevailing usurpers over mankind, superstition and tyranny." Nothing could be hoped from them; and Milton turned from them with the revulsion of contemptuous disgust.

> And what the people but a herd confus'd,
> A miscellaneous rabble, who extol
> Things vulgar, and, well weigh'd, scarce worth the praise?
> They praise and they admire they know not what,
> And know not whom, but as one leads the other;
> And what delight to be by such extoll'd,
> To live upon their tongues, and be thir talk?
> Of whom to be disprais'd were no small praise—
> His lot who dares be singularly good.

And, as if the idea were an obsession, Milton returns to it in *Samson*, where his words are those of the fiercest contempt:

> Nor do I name of men the common rout,
> That wandring loose about
> Grow up and perish, as the summer flie,
> Heads without name no more remembered.

The change in Milton's theological thought is not the least important aspect of the evolution with which we are dealing. We have already seen enough of Milton's ethics to know that if they were a true reflection of his Christianity, he must needs have been a Pelagian in 1640; for he attributes far greater excellence and moral perfection to the individual than even Pelagius did.

Yet we find Milton very orthodox in all his references to theological doctrine before 1655. In the *Reformation Touching Church Discipline* (1641), the following passage occurs:

Thou, therefore, that sittest in light and glory unapproachable, Parent of angels and men! next, thee I implore, omnipotent King, Redeemer of that lost remnant whose nature thou didst assume, ineffable and everlasting Love! and thou, the third subsistence of the divine infinitude, illuminating Spirit, the joy and solace of created things! one Tripersonal godhead!

From this apostrophe we learn that Milton ostensibly accepted not only the orthodox Trinity but also the doctrine of absolute monergism; Christ is the "Redeemer of that lost remnant whose nature thou didst assume." In an early tract, we find high praise for the Council of

Nice.[19] In the pamphlet *Of Prelatical Episcopacy*, Milton rules Tertullian out as an authority to whom the bishops may appeal, because he made "an imparity between God the Father and God the Son." This, however, was precisely what Milton himself later did very deliberately and at great length.[20] In *Defence* of 1651, Milton says, "Mocking the spirit of God is an inexpiable crime." This also is denied in the *Christian Doctrine*.[21] Furthermore, in all the early pamphlets there is abundant evidence to show that Milton at least nominally accepted the current theories of absolute predestination and human depravity.[22] Like all others, he condemns the Pelagians, Arians, etc. In the *Areopagitica* he says that "the acute and distinct Arminius was perverted." Milton had probably read Arminius at least a little, because "acute and distinct" are the best possible descriptive words applicable to his argumentation. That Milton ostensibly condemned Arminius we learn from the fore-

[19] *P. W.*, II, 376.

[20] Cf. entire chap. v, *Christian Doctrine*. The following passages are explicit statements of Milton's teaching: "Again, the Son acknowledges and declares openly, that the Father is greater than the Son." "Since, therefore, the Son derives his essence from the Father, he is posterior to the Father not merely in rank, ... but also in essence."

[21] Milton says: "If to sin against the Holy Spirit . . . . were an unpardonable sin, the Spirit would truly be greater than the Father and the Son." Cf. above, p. 119.

[22] Cf. *P. W.*, II, 371, 448, 492; III, 4, 136, 160, 223–24. In the last passage, he refers to pagan writers to support a blundering defense of the doctrine of preterition. Cf. also *ibid.*, pp. 171, 225, 337–38; V, 24–25, 232, 245; I, 62.

going as well as from another passage[23] in which he insinuates that Bishop Hall was an Arminian, and thus a denier of original sin. This is significant for another reason: it shows that in his early pamphlets Milton had no real comprehension of theological problems; for Arminius by no means denied original sin, nor did he reduce very much the necessity of vicarious atonement or man's universal depravity as taught by Augustine. In his last reference to Arminius, however, Milton shows not only a very different attitude, but also a clear understanding of the issues involved:

The Arminian, lastly, is condemned for setting up free will against free grace; but that imputation he disclaims.

We have called attention to only a few of Milton's particular theological doctrines. But the obvious fact remains that verbally he was always orthodox in his early works and universally heterodox in his maturity; and his heresies are all deliberately formulated and promulgated, and supported by every authority and argument. Are we to assume that Milton, who, in youth, was interested in worldly things only, was then an orthodox Puritan? and that later, when he really entered the two-world sphere, he first became a real heretic? Such a conclusion is evidently absurd.

There is but one logical resolution of the problem: before the Commonwealth, Milton had little knowledge of theology and no interest in the message of Puritanism. He was indifferent to the great doctrines on which it is

[23] *Ibid.*, III, 142.

based, because his interests lay wholly outside its sphere. He was interested in temporal problems—ecclesiastical, political, domestic, intellectual: he cared not at all about the next world. However, he came at a time when theological jargon was the only available vehicle for argumentation, and the sanction of scripture the only valid foundation for belief; if he were to have any effect upon his readers, he would have to assume an external orthodoxy—no deeper than his skin. It is impossible for anyone who understands historical Puritanism even a little to read Milton without observing this fact. Thus it was that under the guise of the narrowest, the most tyrannous, and irrational of all philosophies Milton could demand the most amazingly rational and revolutionary reforms in all departments of human life. He kept his theology and his real thought in separate compartments. He used one for the sake of argument to establish the other.

But, in the course of time, that which had been external became vital: Milton entered the two-world principle of existence. Before this, any doctrine concerning the Trinity, the Incarnation, the Holy Spirit, or Redemption, would do: all were alike indifferent. But afterward the salvation of his own soul became an essential matter, and all the central dogmas of Christianity objects of serious consideration. Milton surrendered a good deal of his independence and self-assertiveness in the change; nevertheless, he lost neither wholly. He found the dogmas wholly contradictory to what he was

prepared to accept; they seemed to him irrational, contradictory, sometimes absurd; they made God utterly
unjust and man a slave; they repudiated absolutely that
human reason upon which Milton had always relied so
much and that human virtue which he had celebrated so
gloriously in *Comus* and the *Areopagitica*. He accepted
the essential elements of Christianity, it is true; he did
not deny that man was a fallen creature, dependent on
grace; he admitted the divine mission of the Saviour and
the need of vicarious atonement. Yet he accepted even
these doctrines only after he had tremendously modified
both them and many others to meet his own needs. To
discuss in detail all the changes he wrought would require a long essay in itself, and would not be very intelli-
gible to the modern reader; but we may say that all of
them were of the same general nature. He made the
whole Christian system rational, that is, such that it
could be comprehended by the human reason and such
that God's justice would be vindicated. He depends
throughout rather upon reason than upon authority; he
gives man both power and responsibility; he reduces the
need for faith and elevates the efficacy of virtuous activity. It is true that Milton's Christianity is of little value
to a dogmatic church, or, indeed, to any church; nor is it
certain that it could be worth anything to many individuals. But it was the natural result when a powerful and
self-reliant pagan mind was converted to Christianity
without altogether losing its paganism. The *Christian
Doctrine* is the step intermediate between the irrational

dogma of Luther and the theology of Harry Emerson Fosdick, which is without creed or dogma altogether.

Milton changed his educational ideal with his interest in theology. The movement, as we would expect, is from paganism to Christianity. In the essay "Of Education" (1644), Christianity plays a very small rôle. It is true that the Bible is to be read at devotionals; but that is wholly beside the main issue. Milton's ideal academy is to produce men "famous to all ages," not because of their religion, but because of their activity in this world. They are to be superb physically, intellectually, and morally—a pagan ideal, diametrically opposed to all that Puritanism stands for. They are to be prepared to become great generals, great statesmen, great philosophers, great artists. The church is practically forgotten. They are to pursue a long and intensive course, based upon pagan models, and consisting mostly of pagan learning; and this is to be consummated by a study of pagan ethics, "the moral works of Plato, Xenophon, Cicero, Plutarch, Laertius, and those Locrian remnants."

But in a pamphlet of 1659, *The Likeliest Means to Remove Hirelings Out of the Church*, we find another interest. It is true that the chief purpose of this work is to persuade the reader against tithes, a state church, and the use of regular temples for worship; in short, Milton wished to make religion feed on a spiritual diet only, and to reduce the worldly income of its ministers to a minimum. But the fact is evident enough that he is here interested in religious rather than in secular education. Every man should possess a copy of "the entire scripture translated into English with plenty of notes; and somewhere or other, I trust, may be found some wholesome body of divinity,[24] as they call it, without school-terms or metaphysical notions, which have obscured rather than explained our religion." There should be many small academies in the country; and at such places those "who intend to be ministers [may be] trained up in the church only by the scripture, and in the original languages thereof." Here, or even in a private house, all requisite learning "either human or divine," may be had. And the sufficient library for a minister may be had for £60. All this is exceedingly economical and practical and was trenchantly severe on the tithe-seeking priests, the Presbyterians, who had once condemned the avaricious bishops, the "blind mouths" of "Lycidas." Nonetheless, it indicates Milton's increased interest in religion for its own sake and his implied renunciation of an ambitious pagan culture.

We will notice but one more aspect of evolution in Milton's thought—that in his ethics. We have already observed the principles of the *Areopagitica* and, to some extent, those of *Comus*. We notice in this masque that man is not only free, self-dependent, the author of his own fate, but also that heaven is his servant. Some there are who,

[24] Can we doubt that Milton was here thinking that perhaps his own *Christian Doctrine* might prove acceptable for this purpose?

> Confin'd, and pester'd in this pinfold here,
> Strive to keep up a frail, and Feaverish being,
> Unmindful of the crown that Vertue gives,
> After this mortal change, to her true Servants
> Amongst the enthron'd gods on Sainted seats.

The Attendant Spirit continues:

> Yet som there be that by due steps aspire
> To lay their just hands on that Golden Key
> That ope's the Palace of Eternity:
> To such my errand is.

Notice that the aid which heaven gives the virtuous man has nothing to do with inducing the virtue itself; the aid so given is purely the result of human excellence:

> So dear to Heav'n is Saintly chastity,
> That when a soul is found sincerely so
> A thousand liveried Angels lacky her.

And again:

> Mortals, that would follow me,
> Love Vertue, she alone is free;
> She can teach you how to clime
> Higher than the Spheary chime.
> Or if Vertue feeble were,
> Heav'n itself would stoop to her.

These ethics, translated into theology, would necessitate an extreme Pelagianism; and yet during his early period Milton seems to condemn Arminius!

In *Paradise Lost,* however, we find a different religious ethic. It is true that the theory of internality still remains, but it has received a vastly modified interpretation. It is the internal that determines one's status and happiness. But that only which is in accordance with law, in harmony with God, is good. Whoever, therefore, like Satan, attempts to depend wholly upon himself, to separate himself from God, is evil; and his internal condition is such that it destroys all possible happiness for the individual. This is a philosophical theory which does, indeed, confer upon the good man autonomy and happiness; but, in comparison with the doctrine of *Comus*, it is one requiring comparative subjection. The fact is that in *Comus* the individual is everything, and God the merest shadow; in *Paradise Lost*, God or the cosmical law swallows up the finite creature and confers freedom and happiness upon him under certain conditions only. This philosophical theory is carried into Milton's mature theology, and is stated in terms of it again and again:

> Man shall not quite be lost, but sav'd who will;
> Yet not of will in him, but grace in me
> Freely voutsaft; once more I will renew
> His lapsèd powers, though forfeit, and enthrall'd
> By sin to foul exorbitant desires:
> Upheld by me, yet once more he shall stand
> On even ground against his mortal foe—
> By me upheld, that he may know how frail
> His fall'n condition is, and to me ow
> All his deliv'rance, and to none but me.
>
> .   .   .   .
> .   .   .   .   I will cleer their senses dark,
> What may suffice, and soft'n stonie hearts
> To pray, repent, and bring obedience due.

To prayer, repentance, and obedience due,
Though but endeavord with sincere intent,
Mine eare shall not be slow, mine eye not shut.
And I will place within them as a guide
My Umpire Conscience; whom if they will hear,
Light after light well us'd they shall attain,
And to the end persisting, safe arrive.
This my long sufferance and my day of grace
They who neglect and scorn, shall never taste;
But hard be hard'nd, blind be blinded more,
That they may stumble on, and deeper fall;
And none but such from mercy I exclude.
But yet all is not don. Man disobeying,
Disloyal breaks his fealtie, and sinns,
Against the high Supremacie of Heav'n,
Affecting Godhead, and so loosing all,
To expiate his Treason hath naught left,
But to destruction sacred and devote,
He with his whole posteritie must die;—
Die hee or Justice must; unless for him
Som other, able, and as willing, pay
The rigid satisfaction, death for death.

This is a fair statement of the Christian theory of
vicarious atonement. But it is the most extreme presentation of it that Milton ever makes, and is softened by
others in which he stresses man's strength rather than
his weakness. The following applies to the state of man
before the Fall; but, as we learn from various passages[25]
both in the *Christian Doctrine* and *Paradise Lost,* it

[25] Cf. *ibid.,* pp. 124 ff. Milton maintains that Christ's satisfaction
was made equally for all mankind (*P. W.,* IV, 314) and that sufficient
grace is thus freely offered to all (*ibid.,* p. 64). Together with this universal grace, there is given to all "the power of volition, that is, of act-

holds true now also with only a modification in degree.
Man is in

> his happie State secure,
> Secure from outward force.

In *Paradise Regained*, we find the heathen philosophers, from whom Milton drew so much, and whom he
praised so enthusiastically during his youth, condemned
because they depend upon human reason and are not,
like the Hebrew prophets, inspired by God. Satan praises
the gentile learning and philosophy, telling Jesus that he
must become acquainted with their ethical doctrines, if
he means to rule by persuasion, as it seemed he intended:

> These rules will render thee a King compleat
> Within thy self.

But Christ, now condemning—albeit for a different reason—that which Comus, the foul and sensual magician,
had once denounced, replies:

> Think not but that I know these things, or, think
> I know them not; not therefore am I short
> Of knowing what I aught: he who receives
> Light from above, from the fountain of light,
> No other doctrine needs, though granted true;
> But these are false, or little else but dreams,
> Conjectures, fancies, built on nothing firm.[26]

. . . .

ing freely in consequence of recovering the liberty of the will by the
renewing of the spirit" (*ibid.*, p. 62). Cf. also: *ibid.*, pp. 266, 284, 324,
325–26, 367. Milton says that in regeneration "our own co-operation
is uniformly required" (*ibid.*, p. 345).

[26] In the lines omitted, Christ condemns successively Socrates,
Plato, the Skeptics, the Epicureans, and the Stoics.

> Alas! what can they teach, and not mislead;
> Ignorant of themselves, of God much more,
> And how the World began, and how Man fell,
> Degraded by himself, on grace depending?
> Much of the Soul they talk, but all awrie;
> And in themselves seek vertue; and to themselves
> All glory arrogate, to God give none.

So far, by 1667, had Milton left behind him his ethics of forty years before. Man must now receive "light from above, from the fountain of light." And no man who is ignorant of the Fall or of his own dependence on grace can teach anything of value. To seek virtue within is to arrogate glory to ourselves and to despise God, and "philosophic pride" must now be avoided as a gangrene of the spirit. Milton here expresses the Christian attitude.

Nevertheless, again, we must not interpret the lines just quoted as containing his exclusive teaching; for the arguments by which Christ refutes Satan in the second book, Milton had learned from those pagans whom he passed such severe judgment upon in the fourth; and the Christ of *Paradise Regained* is one whom Pelagius might well have accepted and whom William Ellery Channing did accept. So inexorable were the demands of Puritan dogma that Milton could not escape the subtle contradiction just indicated.

But it is again in *Samson Agonistes* that we find the completion of the evolution. In *Comus* the individual is an absolutely independent unit; in *Paradise Lost* his happiness depends upon his union and harmony with

God. But in *Samson* Milton surrenders to the unseen without question or protest. Here he condemns those who find God's ways not just,

> As to his own edicts found contradicting;[27]
> Then give the rains to wandring thought,
> Regardless of his glories diminution,
> Till by thir own perplexities involv'd,
> They ravel more, still less resolv'd,
> But never find self-satisfying solution.

This is the result when man tries to understand the counsel of God. And the Chorus continues:

> Down, Reason, then; at least, vain reasonings down.

The uttermost of hopelessness and misery in human life is realized by Samson:

> Nature within me seems
> In all her functions weary of herself;
> My race of glory run, and race of shame,
> And I shall shortly be with them that rest.

> My griefs not only pain
> As a lingering disease,
> But finding no redress, ferment and rage;
> Nor less than wounds immedicable
> Ranckle, and fester, and gangrene,
> To black mortification.
> Thoughts, my Tormenters, arm'd with deadly stings,
> Mangle my apprehensive tenderest parts,
> Exasperate, exulcerate, and raise

[27] The allusion, of course, is to the doctrine of predestination; Calvin said that God determined even the Fall; but most theologians said that Adam had free will up to that time.

> Dire inflammation which no cooling herb
> Or medicinal liquor can asswage,
> Nor breath of Vernal Air from snowy Alp.
> Sleep hath forsook and given me o're
> To deaths benumming Opium as my only cure;
> Thence faintings, swounings of despair,
> And sense of heav'ns desertion.

> Nor am I in the list of them that hope;
> Hopeless are all my evils, all remediless.
> This one prayer yet remains, might I be heard,
> No long petition—speedy death,
> The close of all my miseries, and the balm.

Samson is in the depths of despair because he has been flung from the pinnacle of fortune into the abyss of degradation; and he is in a quandary, a misery of mental conflict, for he cannot see the justice of God's ways. He is one

> Though not disordinate, yet causless suffring
> The punishment of dissolute days. In fine
> Just or unjust alike seem miserable,
> For oft alike, both come to evil end.

The ways of God to man Milton no longer tries to explain: they are past finding out, just as Augustine said. The final religious ethic of Milton is contained in the following passage, put into the mouth of the Chorus:

> God of our Fathers! what is Man,
> That thou towards him with hand so various—
> Or might I say contrarious?—
> Temperst thy providence through his short course:
> Not evenly, as thou rul'st
> The Angelic orders, and inferiour creatures mute,

Irrational and brute?
Nor do I name of men the common rout,
That wandring loose about
Grow up and perish, as the summer flie,
Heads without name no more rememberd;
But such as thou hast solemnly elected,
With gifts and graces eminently adorn'd,
To some great work, thy glory,
And peoples safety, which in part they effect:
Yet toward these, thus dignifi'd, thou oft,
Amidst thir highth of noon,
Changest thy countenance and thy hand with no regard
Of highest favours past
From thee on them, or them to thee of service.
        Nor only dost degrade them, or remit
To life obscur'd, which were a fair dismission,
But throw'st them lower than thou didst exalt them high—
Unseemly falls in human eie,
Too grievous for the trespass or omission;
Oft leav'st them to the hostile sword
Of Heathen and profane, thir carkasses
To dogs and fowls a prey, or else captiv'd:
Or to the unjust tribunals, under change of times,
And condemnation of the ingrateful multitude.
If these they scape, perhaps in poverty
With sickness and disease thou bow'st them down,
Painful diseases and deform'd,
In crude old age.[28]

Nevertheless, the drama has a happy conclusion; all
is joy and victory at the end:

No time for lamentation now,
Nor much more cause.

[28] It is difficult not to read autobiographical significance into this
passage.

Human insight could not perceive the glorious dénouement of the tragedy; the "highest dispensation" indeed "had ends beyond [our] reach to know." Man cannot see the future, or know what is to come. It is foolish for him to attempt to construct any rational philosophy of action by which to guide himself. He must not depend upon himself, but upon God. This is the message of *Samson Agonistes*. If we but throw ourselves upon God with unquestioning faith, all will terminate happily. God sometimes seems

> to hide his face,
> But unexpectedly returns.

Truly, from

> The sun-clad power of Chastity,

which Milton proclaims in *Comus*, to

> God of our Fathers! what is man,

the step is long, and the call is far.

That there is a distinct evolution in almost every aspect of Milton's interest and thinking must be evident; and it remains to give one or two major reasons for the development.

The most important cause for the change I take to be Milton's defeat. We have already seen that the Hellenic philosophy, which was Milton's during youth, is, above all, one of action and victory; and that the Augustinian, which he later accepted with his own alterations of it, is eminently one of surrender, defeat, and consolation. When this world yields nothing but disappointment and despair, man turns inevitably to the unseen. The latter, of course, is purely the product of imagination, and he who accepts its existence is at liberty to embellish it with all glory and magnificence, as well as with corresponding torture and horror. When every thing worth while in the ancient world was going into destruction, Christianity spread rapidly; its message was precisely suited to the moral needs of a fearfully decadent world. What occurred on a vast scale in the Roman Empire occurred on a small one in the mind of John Milton. But an additional factor is to be considered in the latter case: Milton not only found the conceptual world created complete and ready for his acceptance, but it was pressed upon him so urgently by all forces active about him that it required a complete panoply of Stoicism to keep clear of it even for a time. Within a decade and a half of the *Areopagitica*, however, the thought of that pamphlet no longer represented its author's state of mind. During those fifteen years he had seen himself as completely defeated as is well possible for a man. He had given up his dearest hopes "to embark in a troubled sea of noises and harsh disputes." He had helped to overthrow episcopacy; he had then turned against the Presbyterians—in whom he had before seen much hope—with redoubled fury; he had written against every kind of tyranny of which he knew; he had labored ceaselessly; he had sacrificed his sight with pride and resignation. In 1644 he was full of hope for the English people:

> Methinks I see in my mind a noble and puissant nation rousing herself like a strong man after sleep, and shaking her invincible locks: methinks I see her as an eagle mewing her mighty youth, and kindling her undazzled eyes at the full midday beam.

But this did not last long. The note of disappointment is distinctly sounded in the *Second Defence* (1654); and, in the *Ready and Easy Way* (1659), which was but a despairing political effort, it is far deeper. And this was the last of Milton's endeavors at practical or temporal reform. He retired from the conflict crushed in spirit. He had fought with all his might for the "good old Cause";[29] he had staked everything upon it. Few men in the world are capable of expending as much energy as he had lavished to procure its permanence. A man's disappointment at any failure must be proportionate to his investment; and Milton had given his all. He was utterly defeated. He saw everything for which he had hoped destroyed. The king returned, and with him all the tyranny, corruption, indecency, sycophancy, and frivolity of the royal court; the bishops were also restored; the moral excellence in which he gloried was the mock of every fawning courtier and popular poet or dramatist; his theories of education and divorce were treated with scorn; the intellectual freedom he had demanded was overwhelmed by a new censorship which

[29] As the Commonwealth was called, and as Milton calls it (*P. W.*, II, 138). Cf. Dryden, *Absalom and Achitophel*, Part I, l. 82.

realized what he foretold in the *Areopagitica*. His treatise on divinity would have been proscribed by the authorities had they not prevented its publication. His poetry found little acceptance. He was himself almost totally forgotten. Was ever a great life so utterly wasted as Milton's must have seemed to him to be? Yet amidst the general destruction of all that he held good and sacred, he drew himself up in lonely majesty[30] and poured forth his soul into a poem which is one of the world's supreme monuments to genius. Yet it reflects a great defeat—the defeat which was its author's greatest experience in life.

Let it not be thought, however, that this vast disappointment was either permanently to be realized or anything even to be regretted. Within fifty years Milton was well on the way toward coming into his own, and since then he has lost no ground; he has been for two centuries and a quarter one of the great vital influences in the English-speaking world. And the depth and permanent value of his message are the direct result of that experience which he considered a final defeat, so far as this world is concerned. A deep distress humanized his soul. Such conceptions as we find basic in *Paradise Lost* would have been impossible had not their author been through the storm and stress of conflict. Furthermore, peace and leisure came only with defeat; then only could the

[30] Wordsworth has given us a very accurate description of Milton in his sonnet, which is worth careful study: Milton's "soul *was* like a star and dwelt apart."

Celestial Light
Shine inward, and the mind through all her powers
Irradiate.

Without the struggle, the defeat, and the consequent re-
tirement, which constitute the story of Milton's life
from 1640 to 1660, he could never have given us *Paradise Lost*.

But this is a digression. There is one more reason
for the evolution of Milton's thought—the immeasura-
ble tyranny which Puritan dogma exercised over the
minds of men in Milton's day. The combined effect of
skepticism, rationalism, higher criticism, and scientific
investigation of natural phenomena is now such that we
can have no conception of the ordinary attitude with
which Milton's contemporaries approached the dogmas
of the church. It would be impossible today to put forth
any proposition half so shocking to the American people
as were the doctrines of universal grace and free will to
the average Puritan—and of these the ordinary modern layman has never heard. To demand the death of
Charles I was indeed horrible, for his person was holy;
and we know that he was executed contrary to the wishes
of almost all Englishmen and that a book purporting to
be written by "his sacred majesty" was, for a time, the
most popular ever published in England.[31] For many
decades afterward the Commonwealth was regarded
with great horror and kings with equal veneration. For

[31] The *Eikon Basiliké* went through more than fifty editions in one
year.

Milton to attack the King was, we say, an act of fearful temerity; but to impugn the orthodox teachings in regard to religion was immeasurably more so. That was to insult God, to endanger the eternal welfare of countless souls. Such ideas were so deeply fixed in the minds of men that we can now have no adequate comprehension of their tyranny. And Milton had no such aids to combat church dogma as the modern unbeliever possesses; he had nothing but his ethical principles and his natural understanding; and even these were cowed by his personal experience and his later religious needs.

Thus we have reviewed the various aspects of evolution in Milton's thought. This is indeed more complex and profound than what took place in the minds of Gascoigne, Wither, Vaughan, Donne, Hall, Dryden, and Newman; yet it is fundamentally similar. We find throughout Milton that the tendency is from paganism toward Christianity; from absolute to qualified self-reliance, and, at last, to surrender; from light theorizing to profound and fundamental conceptions; from delight in, to disappointment with, this world; and from sensuous beauty to cosmical philosophy. Thus it is that we find so many elements in Milton: he is neither pagan nor Christian; nor is he both. He is himself; and his message is simply and finally "Miltonic."

CHAPTER V

THE MESSAGE OF PARADISE LOST

A considerable volume might be compiled of criticism concerning Milton's Satan and the purpose of *Paradise Lost*. But in spite of the fact that the Archfiend is obviously central in his setting, no one seems yet to have realized that the purpose of the epic is insepafably involved with its chief character. It would indeed be strange if such were not the case. Furthermore, almost all the criticism thus far advanced in regard either to Satan or to the purpose of *Paradise Lost* has been impressionistic; practically no one has attempted a systematic analysis of the poem in the light of theology and philosophy to discover the bases by which Milton's underlying purposes in writing his epic and in portraying Satan as he did may be comprehended.

It is curious as well as interesting to note what various critics have declared the theme and purpose of *Paradise Lost* to be. Many theories have been advanced, as diverse as they are numerous. Addison was the first in the field; but his naïve statements signalize his failure to understand Puritanism or Milton's masterpiece. Certainly, he did not delve beneath the surface when he declared the theme of that poem to be the Fall of Man and its significance to the whole human race. Samuel Johnson said that Milton first found his moral and then built his poem thereon. This was "to shew the reasonableness of religion, and the necessity of obedience to the Divine Law."[1] There is profundity in this statement. H. Carpenter[2] maintained that it was Milton's purpose to picture, in Satan and his chief angels, the Puritans who were mighty in the councils of the Commonwealth. George E. Woodberry says: "The origin and destiny of the soul and the meaning of its course in history was the real theme of *Paradise Lost*."[3] This illustrates the unmeaning generality which criticism too often becomes. Paul Elmer More, though usually a very acute writer, has the strangest solution of all: "Sin is not the innermost theme of Milton's epic, nor man's disobedience and Fall. . . . . Justification of the ways of God to man is not the true moral of the plot. . . . . The true theme is Paradise itself . . . . the 'happy mural seat,' "[4] where the errant tempter beheld the first human pair in their pristine happiness. John Erskine holds that Milton wished to show how much man was the gainer by his Fall.[5] C. A. Moore—undoubtedly correct as far as he goes—declares[6] that *Paradise Lost* was written to vindicate Providence of the charge of injustice and to substitute a less repulsive Christianity for Calvinism. E. N. S. Thomp-

[1] *Lives of the Poets* (Oxford), I, 122.

[2] *Unitarian Re.*, V, 303.

[3] *Great Writers*, pp. 96–97.

[4] "The True Theme of Paradise Lost," *Indep.*, LIV, 277.

[5] *Publications of the Modern Language Association*, 1917.

[6] *Ibid.*, 1921.

son's statement that Milton's purpose "is to expound the workings of the moral law"[7] has profound implications; but these he fails to realize and goes no farther than to say, "Milton's attention is fixed on his central theme—the origin and course of evil."[8] Denis Saurat—hitting upon significant but partial truth—voluminously maintains that at the bottom of *Paradise Lost* and, for that matter, of Milton's whole philosophy, lies the one great conception that evil is the dominion of passion over reason.[9] Quite contrary to Carpenter and others, Saurat says that in the fall of the evil angels, Milton prophesies the fall of the royalists—who represent passion—and the beginning of the millenium.[10] But this seems rather fantastic, especially as we know that *Paradise Lost* was first planned about 1642.

It is evident that the "solutions" just reviewed are unphilosophical and contradictory in the extreme. It is surely possible to arrive at more recondite conclusions.

Most of what has been written concerning Milton's Satan is equally shallow and uncritical. Satan is a great and sublime figure, the heroic antagonist of God, the great fiend who, in spite of the hopelessness of his conflict with that power "whom thunder hath made greater," continues to fascinate us and to compel our admiration.

[7] *Essays on Milton,* p. 181.   [8] *Ibid.,* p. 182.

[9] *La Pensée de Milton* (Paris, 1920).

[10] Saurat supposes that Milton was a Fifth Monarchist, but this surely is a strange misconception either of Milton or else of the Fifth Monarchy Men. Cf. his *La Pensée.*

Perhaps Milton made Satan so excellent because he was to be the protagonist in a tragedy, and, as such, must not be mean but able to excite our sympathy.[11] At all events, Satan is the central figure and probably the hero of the poem. F. M. Elfresh says, "Properly speaking, there is only one character in *Paradise Lost*."[12] Yet to some he has seemed very bad; Dr. Johnson said, "The malignity of Satan foams in haughtiness and obstinacy." Quite different are the words of P. T. Forsyth: "We fear God, but we like Satan."[13] "Satan represents, as no one in Milton's heaven does, the side of reason, personality, and freedom in conflict with throned force.[14] That Milton's chief sympathy was with Satan seems to be the general conception. But so far as I know, no one has yet made an analysis of the ethics, the metaphysics, and the theology of *Paradise Lost* to discover what Milton had in mind in his portrayal of Satan. Some seem to think that the Archfiend grew under the poet's hands, quite unintentionally, and that Milton unconsciously invested the Devil with all his own pride, egotism, rebelliousness, and love for superiority. Some have even gone so far as to identify Milton's God with Charles II,[15] the fiends with the parliamentary leaders, and Satan with Milton himself.[16] To me it seems that such impressionistic conceptions are scarcely worthy of comment.

[11] Cf. J. E. C. Welldon, *Nineteenth Century*, "The Theology of Milton," LXXI, 903.

[12] *Meth. Re.*, XX, 71.

[13] *Cont. Review*, XCV, 450.   [15] Carpenter, *ibid.*

[14] *Ibid.*, p. 464.   [16] Forsyth, *ibid.*, p. 450.

The following statements are fairly representative
of what has been accepted as the truth about Satan:

It is Milton's art which has invested the character of Satan
with so striking a dignity that, in spite of his treason against the Almighty, he has commanded something of sympathy and even respect from many Christians.[17] Milton's God embodies the resolute
government which makes rebels. Satan bespeaks our sympathies
at the very outset as a rebel against the arbitrary divine decree.[18]
This is no war of Gods and mortals, or even of gods and Titans.
It is god against god.[19] They [Messiah and Satan] were both created beings—Satan possibly the senior. . . . . They were not of
intrinsically different nature.[20]

Emily Hickey,[21] however—although her statement
may be incorrect—makes a real contribution to the discussion by saying that Satan was never meant to be a
hero. This contention she maintains by tracing the
moral degradation and disintegration of the Fiend. She
shows that toward the end of the epic he has become
quite contemptible, and that the process by which he
became so was continuous, gradual, and evidently pre-
determined by the poet.

Denis Saurat has a theory which is nothing if not
original: according to him (quite contrary to the common conception), Satan and Milton are—because they
have so much in common—personal enemies; thus the
poet throughout takes a very keen delight in visiting acrimonious vengeance upon his foe; the hero of the poem

[17] Welldon, *ibid.*, p. 903.
[18] Forsyth, *ibid.*, p. 452.
[19] *Ibid.*, p. 456.
[20] *Ibid.*, p. 458.
[21] *Catholic World*, XCVI, 58–71.

is Milton himself, obtaining a great victory over the devil, who is symbolic of the evil in the poet's own soul:

> The hero of *Paradise Lost* is Milton himself.
>
> Milton throws himself personally into the struggle against Satan, and from the reading of *Paradise Lost* one derives two inevitable impressions: the greatness of Satan and the greatness of Milton. . . . . He it is, and not God or the Son, that overcomes Satan. . . . . He exposes Satan so passionately that he forgets Satan's natural enemies: he takes their place before the enemy. . . . .
>
> Nor was it entirely his egotism, however largely unconscious, that lured him into this attitude. There was a deeper cause: Milton had Satan in him and wanted to drive him out. He had felt passion, pride, and sensuality. The deep pleasure he takes in his creation of Satan is the joy . . . . peculiar to the artist. . . . . Hence that strange monster Satan. Whereas inferior artists build their monsters artificially, Milton takes his, living and warm with his own life, out of himself.[22]

A pretty superstructure, but based on rather flimsy foundations!

Assuredly, these explanations are too narrow, too simple, or too frivolous to explain what lies behind the great poem on which so much genius, learning, labor, and meditation were expended, which even crabbed Dr. Johnson could pronounce the greatest achievement of the human mind, and the purpose of which was to justify the ways of God to men. In the face of the evidence, it is unreasonable to suppose that Milton had no definite plan; and it is absurd to say that he did not or could not

[22] *Milton, Man and Thinker*, p. 220.

execute that plan, that he was carried away by his subject, and that, without conscious intention, Satan grew under his hands, especially when we know that he did not grow but disintegrated. To think that Milton would make *Paradise Lost* a personal or political attack of any kind is to misconceive his character utterly. In concord with his Renaissance esthetic theory,[23] he wrote it to

teach over the whole book of sanctity and virtue, through all the instances of example . . . . that whereas the paths of honesty and good life now appear rugged and difficult, though they be indeed easy and pleasant, they will then appear to all men both easy and pleasant though they were rugged and difficult indeed.

He hoped that his work would make him "famous to all ages." Even in his most fiery pamphlets—those which concern divorce and press censorship—he lays aside all immediately personal considerations and deals only with fundamental and general principles. Yet, in these cases, there was a direct personal application. In both the *Christian Doctrine* and *Paradise Lost,* however, no immediate issue was involved. He spoke like a great teacher addressing the *intellectuelles* of all succeeding generations, "a fit audience though few," that is, comparatively few. The belief that Milton embodied anything in his chef d'oeuvre not supremely philosophical and universal is absurd.

Before we can come to any understanding as to what Milton intended to teach in his portrayal of Satan, we must realize certain facts: first, that Satan's character

[23] Cf. Sidney's *Defense of Poesy* (edited by A. S. Cook), pp. 20–25.

undergoes a progressive desiccation and degradation; second, that good angels, fiends, and men are all alike in kind—differing but in degree—but are different in *kind* from the Word or Messiah; third, that there is no such thing as a struggle between God (or Messiah) and Satan; fourth, that, in all ordinary points of comparison, the devils in general and Satan in particular are immensely superior to human beings. Our problem, then, is clearly defined: after establishing the above-mentioned facts, we may interpret Milton's teaching concerning Satan in the light of his relationship to God and Messiah, and through our understanding of the nature of good, evil, and sin in the individual, finite being, and in the universe as a whole.

As Satan's progressive degradation has already been recognized,[24] we need not discuss this as fully as might otherwise be necessary. This process is evidently the result of careful forethought on the part of the poet. At the beginning of *Paradise Lost,*

> His form had not yet lost
> All her Original brightness, nor appeer'd
> Less than Arch Angel ruind, and the excess
> Of glory Obscur'd.

Satan was not yet far from his primal excellence in point of time; and his strength, majesty, and glory had only begun to wither, to become obscured. Physically, intellectually, morally, he appears, in the first book of *Par-*

[24] Cf. also P. T. Forsyth, *ibid.;* and E. N. S. Thompson, *Essays on Milton, ibid.,* pp. 184–86.

adise Lost, beyond peer. He relies upon his own resources; he is straightforward; he commands the fallen
host by merit of power and integrity; he seeks no sub-
terfuges; he admits his accidental defeat, but not, ostensibly, his inferiority. It is because of all this that
Satan has aroused so much sympathy in his own behalf.

But we must notice that even from the beginning of
their imprisonment in hell, the angels tacitly admit the
superiority of God. Beëlzebub, for example, says:

> Leader of those Armies bright,
> Which, but th' Omnipotent, none could have foyled.

God, then, possesses *all* power, being "omnipotent."
And later Satan himself admits that they did not before
know the strength of God, because he concealed it.[25]
Therefore,

> Our better part remains
> To work in close design, by fraud or guile,
> What force effected not.

This is the point of departure. Satan here admits the impossibility of meeting God in the open; he resolves to
use guile, deceit, treachery—the weapons of the weak
and contemptible—to accomplish his designs. The moral
effect of this upon him who does it is most deleterious.
He sinks into cowardice, slavery, and utter despica-
bility.

The principal fiends all admit God's absolute sov-
ereignty: Moloch can offer no better hope from war

[25] *Paradise Lost,* I, 637-44.

against heaven than annihilation; Belial is certain that
God can without the least effort repel all their attacks
upon the crystal battlements, and increase their hellish
tortures at will; and Mammon says:

> For he, be sure,
> In highth or depth, still first and last will Reign
> Sole King.

And Beëlzebub adds:

> Heav'n, whose high walls fear no assault or Siege
> Or ambush from the Deep.

I have been thus full concerning this matter, because it
is from his realization of the impossibility of combat-
ing God that Satan proposes the use of fraud to compass
a spiteful, contemptible, and self-degrading revenge. In
accomplishing this, he is compelled to use methods which
make him in the end incomparably pitiful.

In obtaining egress from hell, Satan, for the first
time in his existence, resorts to hypocrisy. At first, he
tries to cowe Death into fear and obedience; but he finds
this impracticable:

> The subtle Fiend his lore
> Soon learned . . . . and thus answerd smooth:
> Dear Daughter—since thou claim'st me for thy Sire,
> And my fair Son here showst me. . . . .

Hypocrisy and guile now become the ordinary means
by which Satan accomplishes his ends: arriving at the
Sun, he accosts its regent, Uriel, in the guise of a minor
angel of light:

> So spake the false dissembler unperceivd;
> For neither Man nor Angel can discern
> Hypocrisie—the only evil that walks
> . Invisible, except to God alone.

In the beginning of the fourth book, Satan first begins to feel the internal misery, which is the result of his degradation:

> Me miserable! which way shall I flie
> Infinite wrauth, and infinite despaire?
> Which way I flie is Hell; my self am Hell;
> And in the lowest deep, a lower deep
> Still threatning to devour me opens wide
>
> .   .   .   .
>
> The lower still I fall, only supreme
> In misery.

A little later we find Satan filled with envy and hatred —degrading and contemptible passions—at the sight of Adam and Eve. His countenance has been seen by one of the celestial guardians "with passions foul obscured." He is found by Zephon and Ithuriel "squat like a toad," inducing into the mind of Eve, in this despicable fashion, sinful fancies. When he is touched by the spear of Ithuriel, Satan assumes his natural likeness and is called the "griesly King." Again, as at hell-gate, he assumes a bold front, but he is soon abashed, this time by two minor angels; Lucifer is no longer the majestic being who fought almost upon terms of equality with Michael on the celestial champaign. He was especially disconcerted

> to find here observed
> His lustre visibly impair'd.

And when, a little later still, he meets Gabriel he falls to lying, subterfuge, hypocrisy, dissimulation, and self-contradiction. He has become an intellectual coward and is dishonest even with himself. When Satan sees "his mounted scale aloft," he admits his own comparative impotence in the most spectacular manner possible by fleeing silently and precipitantly. He is now degraded immeasurably below what he was when he fought in heaven, or even when he presided over the infernal peers in the council of Pandemonium.

In the ninth book, Satan's misery and degradation have become greater still:

> And the more I see
> Pleasures about me, so much more I feel
> Torment within me, as from the hateful siege
> Of contraries; all good to me becomes
> Bane, and in Heav'n much worse would be my state.
>
> O foul descent! that I who erst contended
> With God to sit the highest, am now constrained
> Into a Beast, and mixt with bestial slime,
> This essence to incarnate and imbrute,
> That to the hight of Deity aspir'd!
>
> . . . .
> Revenge, at first though sweet,
> Bitter ere long back on itself recoiles.

Satan, in his cowardice, attacks the woman, and not Adam "whose higher intellectual more I shun." He won his point over Eve by means of glozing hypocrisy, lying, flattery—all that is contemptible. And when Eve tasted the apple,

> Back to the Thicket slunk
> The guiltie Serpent.

Satan's work of deceit now being over, he returns to hell, where he experiences "joyless triumphals." He comes clad

> With what permissive glory since his fall
> Was left him, or false glitter.

Upon completion of his boasting speech, he hears, instead of universal applause, an universal hiss; and when the serpent-fiends expect to slake their thirst by means of apples, they chew bitter ashes and dust.

Furthermore—and this is very important—Satan has now passed the stage in which defiance of God is any longer possible. He not only accepts God's omnipotence and the justness of his own fate,[26] but he has lost all hope of avoiding the particular sentence that has been pronounced upon him.[27] He finds temporary consolation in the hope of delay. Satan's self-assertiveness and Stoic self-sufficiency have wholly vanished.

In *Paradise Regained* we find Satan far more despicable than even at the close of *Paradise Lost*. He is in a quandary of fear and uncertainty, filled with memory of past defeat and fear of impending punishment. He must use, he says,

> Not force, but well-couch't fraud, well-woven snares.

He is no longer the angel or the Archfiend; he is only a pitiable, devilish, wily little imp, full of hypocrisy and

---

[26] *Ibid.*, IV, 41–101.   [27] *Ibid.*, X, 496–501.

dissimulation. He employs the utmost of his art; but Jesus, who has nothing but human reason with which to withstand it, conquers easily. It may even be said that *Paradise Regained* is fundamentally uninteresting because the forces of evil are altogether inconsiderable—even despicable. Jesus sees the fact—too clearly to make dramatic interest possible—that

> lying is thy sustence, thy food.

Satan is foiled at every turn; Jesus analyzes his argument, and, with merciless logic, points out its fallacy. In the light of understanding—human reason—Satan is revealed in his true colors. He who fought on even terms with archangels is now defeated with ease, in the moral realm, by a man! What humiliation and misery was this!

In all literature there is no other example of moral degradation and desiccation equal to that in Milton's Satan.

The next fact we must realize is that angels (both good and bad) and men are alike in kind; but that all of these differ in kind from God or the Word.

When Milton was describing the fiends in hell, he was portraying beings who have character—that is, a complex of moral traits, such as ambition, fear, hope, love, hatred, and desire for revenge, glory, domination, riches, etc.—precisely as we find in human beings. For this reason, as Dr. Johnson noticed,[28] there is considera-

---

[28] *Lives of the Poets,* I, 123.

ble diversity among the evil angels. Like human beings, they react variously to external stimuli. And the reason that Milton made his fiends so much like human beings is that they belong to the same general order of creation. The fiends were fallen angels; we are fallen men. The same moral qualities exist in both.

That men and angels belong to the same order of created beings is clearly explained by Raphael in two passages of *Paradise Lost,* which we have already quoted.[29] We learn here that angels differ from men chiefly in that the former are spiritual—instead of material— and purely intelligential—instead of rational,

> Differing but in degree, of kind the same.

In all existence, there is an endless scale of things, all, however, "one first matter." Spirit is only matter etherealized; and *intuitive* reason (that which perceives truth instantaneously) is only a keener reason than the discursive (that which arrives at conclusions by logical processes). All things in nature feed upon and contain all the forms of existence lower than themselves in the ladder of being. Thus angels have all the qualities of men, but men can develop themselves into angels, just as stalks grow from roots, leaves from stalks, fruit from flowers; just as vital spirits develop into animal, and these in turn into intellectual. Because this metaphysical system is the groundwork of all existence, Raphael could eat of Adam's proffered meal with

> real hunger, and concoctive heate
> To transubstantiate.

[29] *Paradise Lost,* V, 404–16, 472–512.

Nowhere, perhaps, does Milton better indicate the near equality of man and angel than in the fourth book of *Paradise Lost:* it is here evident that the fallen angel feels himself inferior to unfallen man, and therefore dares not attack him. Satan soliloquizes; he describes Adam as

> Heroic built, though of terrestrial mould;
> Foe not informidable, exempt from wound—
> I not; so much hath Hell debas'd, and paine
> Infeebl'd me, to what I was in Heaven.

Unfallen angel is superior to faithful man, as is also fiend to fallen man; but man upright is stronger in himself than angel degenerate.

The actions of the fiends in their diversions, in their battles with each other, in the building of Pandemonium, etc., all indicate their affinity with human beings. The fiends are creatures, and when they accomplish anything they can employ only those physical means which are commensurate with their individual strength. The angels are indeed greater, more powerful, and more intellectual entities than we, but they differ from us much as the most powerful of us differs from the weakest. When Satan goes on his journey to the earth, the fallen angels have Olympic games: they have tournaments and chariot races; some indulge in feats of physical strength. Others set out on ambitious journeys to explore hell. When the angels of Michael battle with the angels of Lucifer in heaven, they perform no actions without physical agency; they use swords, shields, cannon; they use hills, with their pines and streams upon them, as projectiles. They are, however, only doing in a vast way what mortals do in a slight way. Pandemonium is truly a building far greater and more magnificent than anything builded by man, but it is erected in the same way as we erect our great structures. Physical force is used; ore is mined and smelted; no action is immediate or by fiat. *The fiends have no supernatural power*. In truth, Milton recognizes no such power, for even the work of creation is strictly natural with the Deity, as is Raphael's speed with an angel of light. Every effect is the inevitable result of some adequate cause. When Satan "wings the desolate Abyss," he is doing nothing contrary to physical law. This is no greater feat for him than swimming the English Channel is for a human being. He must struggle with and overcome physical obstacles, just as every one who is to win a notable victory must also do.

We notice, furthermore, that the intellectual and esthetic interests of the fiends are the same as those of men. Some sing mellifluous melodies to angelic strains of music; while others,

> sat on a Hill retir'd,
> In thoughts more elevate, and reason'd high
> Of Providence, Foreknowledge, Will, and Fate—
> Fixt Fate, free will, foreknowledge absolute
> And found no end, in wandring mazes lost.
> Of good and evil much they argu'd then,
> Of happiness and final misery,
> Passion and Apathie, and glory and shame.

Everything that human beings can do, the devils do; but in every point of comparison the fiends are in-

variably far superior to men. Milton more than hints at
these facts in the following passages:

> For neither do the Spirits damn'd
> Loose all their vertue; least bad men should boast
> Thir specious deeds on earth, which glory excites
> Or close ambition, varnisht o're with zeal.

> O shame to men! Devil with Devil damn'd
> Firm concord holds; men onely disagree
> Of Creatures rational, though under hope
> Of heavenly Grace; and God proclaiming peace,
> Yet live in hatred, enmitie, and strife,
> Among themselves.

When, however, we consider Messiah, or the Word,
we find that we are dealing with an altogether different
order of being. His acts are immediate, and he accomplishes his ends without process or agency, but by mere
fiat. After the faithful angels have fought with the apos-
tate for three days without any satisfactory conclusion,
the Word seats himself in the Chariot of Paternal Deity
and issues forth to the field of conflict:

> Before him Power Divine the way prepar'd;
> At his command the uprooted Hills retir'd
> Each to his place; they heard his voice, and went
> Obsequious.

> One Spirit in them[30] rul'd, and every eye
> Glar'd lightning, and shot forth pernicious fire
> Among th' accurst, that witherd all thir strength,
> And of thir wonted vigour left them draind,
> Exhausted, spiritless, afflicted, fallen.

[30] That is, in the four cherubic shapes that drew the chariot.

> Yet half his strength he put not forth, but check'd
> His Thunder in mid Volie; for he meant
> Not to destroy, but root them out of Heav'n.
> The overthrown he rais'd, and as a heard
> Of Goats or timerous flocks together throng'd,
> Drove them before him Thunder-struck, pursu'd
> With terrors and with Furies to the bounds
> And Chrystall wall of Heav'n; which, op'ning wide,
> Rowld inward, and a spacious Gap disclos'd
> Into the Wasteful Deep. The monstrous sight
> Strook them with horror backward, but far worse
> Urg'd them behind; headlong themselves they threw
> Down from the verge of Heav'n: Eternal wrauth
> Burnt after them to the bottomless pit.

There is no better way, perhaps, to illustrate the difference between the finite and the infinite than by comparing the way in which the Word wrought the new universe and that in which the angels constructed Pandemonium. The latter is the result of great ingenuity and much physical labor. But the world is brought into existence by fiat, just as the hills were commanded to their place again. Messiah merely gives commands to Chaos, and the new universe comes into being: thus does God "put forth [his] goodness":

> So spake th' Almightie: and to what he spake
> The Word, the Filial Godhead, gave effect.
> Immediate are the Acts of God, more swift
> Than time or motion.

The Word speaks:

> Silence, ye troubl'd waves, and, thou Deep, peace!

"Chaos heard his voice."

God is the creator; angels and men are mere laborers
and mechanics—albeit sometimes very ingenious ones.

✕   Partially from what has already been established,
we must now realize that between God and Satan there
cannot properly be said to be any *struggle* at all. Satan,
indeed—for a while—attempts to deny his defeat and
his fate. Nevertheless, before God's omnipotence, Satan
is but a sapling in the pathway of the onrushing ava-
lanche. In regard to mere might, Satan is immeasurably
less in comparison with God or the Word than the tini-
est of the whole creation is in comparison with the greatest. It is this that Satan first tries to deny; but which,
as we have already seen, he soon realized and candidly
admitted. With respect to power, then, human and angelic creatures are both, in comparison with God, utterly
infinitesimal. They are both so far beneath him that he
can scarcely discern any difference between them. He
says:

> What thinkst thou then of mee and this my State?
> Seem I to thee sufficiently possest
> Of happiness, or not, who am alone
> From all Eternitie? for none I know
> Second to mee or like, equal much less.
> How have I then with whom to hold converse,
> Save with the Creatures which I made, and those
> To me inferiour infinite descents
> Beneath what other Creatures are to thee?

But even though their might be unutterably inconse-
quential, men and angels are both of tremendous signifi-

cance because of other qualities which they do possess and which render them, in a way, like God, "the images of the creator." They possess reason and free will; they are independent moral agents; their ultimate fate in the universe depends upon themselves. Therefore, in every created soul there is enacted a moral drama, individual in its nature, and paramount in its significance. The might of God never effects in any way the outcome of the struggle, which is of eternal consequence. As long as they maintain their own moral integrity, which is a purely internal matter, they are absolutely invulnerable to all attack from without. For this reason, the finite being need never fear force, but only guile, which seeks to destroy his moral excellence. It is thus that Satan achieves the ruin of Adam and Eve. Lucifer was the most admirable and elevated of all finite existences in the universe. At the end of *Paradise Regained* the moral tragedy has been played through, and he is exceedingly despicable. What does Milton intend to signify by this? It is evident that he has indicated the effects of sin in a moral agent. This effect can be found in an angel or in a man. Satan recognizes this to have been true of himself, as we find in his soliloquy in the fourth book of *Paradise Lost*. We are particularly interested in the moral drama taking place in the Archfiend because he is, in comparison with man, intrinsically so great and because he was so superbly admirable before his degradation began.

The fact that Satan's character undergoes an extraordinary, progressive desiccation; that angels and men are essentially similar beings; that the fiends are really only superior and ethereal men; that there is no such thing as a struggle between God and a creature; that every finite being is a self-dependent moral unit— all these facts indicate that in the portrayal of Satan we have an ethical philosophy immediately applicable to the human being. But how this application is to be made, we may understand only by reference to Milton's metaphysical principles.

We remember that, according to those principles, God is the material of the cosmos; that he is fate, the willing power, the fundamental spiritual and physical law which governs all portions of the universe; that he is the moral force which enables us to know good from evil; that he is the reverse of chaos, passion, or lawlessness; and that, finally, he is the illuminating and vivifying force that gives life to all existence. God is without personality.

But even though the will of God is destiny, his decrees are so framed as to make the finite individual a free moral agent. The law of God is general and merely makes it necessary that certain effects shall always be the result of certain causes. The result of sin is inevitable moral degradation: this fact is dependent upon the universal order of things, and whoever, therefore, is guilty of sin must undergo its penalty. Whether any individual shall commit sin, however, is a matter which

God has left in his own hands. "The liberty of man," says Milton, is "entirely independent of necessity."

We have already seen that in Milton's metaphysics there is no positive evil. But that which is furthest from God and least like him is least good, the worst state at which anything can arrive. Chaos in the universe is the lowest status possible: it is supreme anarchy, the condition of ultimate negativity.

Milton's conception of evil and good is the key to our understanding of the work, in the universe, of Satan and Messiah. They are diametrically opposed to each other; and their work is carried on both in the cosmos as a whole and separately in all finite creatures. Messiah is called by the Father:

My Word, my Wisdom, and effectual Might.

It is he who creates the new world. In the cosmos it is the business of Messiah, as we have already seen, to construct, to create, to build up, to reduce chaos to law or reason, to bring order out of disorder, to replace darkness by light. And in regard to the human being, his work is precisely parallel; men shall

live in thee transplanted, and from thee
Receive new life.

The work of Jesus is to raise mortals in the scale of existence by persuading them to follow his example. Satan, however, is the direct reverse of all this. It is his objective to do evil:

> But of this be sure—
> To do aught good never will be our task,
> But ever to do ill our sole delight,
> As being the contrary to his high will
> Whom we resist.

And even as good consists in constructive labor—in the raising of objects in the scale of existence—so evil consists in destruction—in reducing them in that scale. We learn this partially from Satan's colloquy with Chaos; the King of Confusion complains that his losses have been heavy:

> I upon my Frontieres here
> Keep residence; if all I can will serve
> That little which is left so to defend,
> Encroacht on still through our intestine broiles
> Weakening the Scepter of old Night: first Hell
> Your dungeon stretching far and wide beneath;
> Now lately Heaven and Earth, another World
> Hung ore my Realm.

It is Satan's avowed purpose *to repair the losses of Chaos,* to reduce law to disorder, to make that evil which has lately become good:

> Direct my course;
> Directed, no mean recompence it brings
> To your behoof, if I that Region lost,
> All usurpation thence expell'd, reduce
> To her original darkness and your sway
> (Which is my present journey), and once more
> Erect the Standerd there of ancient Night.
> Yours be th' advantage all, mine the revenge!

And in regard to man himself, Satan has the same purpose; when Adam and Eve ate of the fruit, they— swayed by passion or lawlessness—simply disregarded the inward divine law—reason or conscience—and did what they knew they should not. As soon as their fall was completed, a state of things prevailed within them— who were microcosms—remarkably similar to that of chaos. It is impossible not to see the obvious parallel between the evil in the universe and the evil in the human heart: *they are the same thing in differing degrees of comprehensiveness.*

> Nor onely Teares
> Raind at thir eyes, but high Winds worse within
> Began to rise, high Passions—Anger, Hate,
> Mistrust, Suspicion, Discord—and shook sore
> Thir inward State of Mind, calm Region once
> And full of Peace, now tost and turbulent;
> For Understanding rul'd not, and the Will
> Heard not her lore, both in subjection now
> To sensual Appetite, who from beneathe
> Usurping over sovran Reason, claimd
> Superior sway.

Thus Satan is the destructive and Messiah the constructive force both in the macrocosm and the microcosm.

In this analysis it is next necessary to realize what Milton means by "sin." (Sin, of course, is any act by which the finite being becomes estranged from God.)

Sin . . . . is ἀνομία, or the transgression of the law. . . . . By the law is here meant . . . . that rule of conscience, which is innate, and engraven upon the mind of man.

Sin, then, is a disregard for the indwelling reason, the image of God—the refusal to obey the Deity. Still more specific is the teaching of *Paradise Lost:*

> Under his great Vicegerent Reign abide,
> United as one individual soule,
> For ever happie. Him who disobeyes,
> Mee disobeyes, breaks union, and that day
> Cast out from God and blessed vision, falls
> Into utter darkness.

Sin, we see, is *separation,* the breaking of unity; it is a denial of the fundamental unity of the pantheistic universe; it is a disregard for the necessary relationship existing between the creator and the created—the infinite and finite. Sin is disharmony with God on the part of man or angel. When Satan rebelled, he denied that he owed his existence to God, that he was ever created at all, and maintained that he was self-begot, that his "puissance [was his] own." He attempted to be a universe unto himself.[31] The war of the "embryon atoms" in chaos was very similar to the intestine conflict which Satan brought in among the creatures in heaven. This separation and disharmony, this breaking of unity, this denial of the profound and essential homogeneity of all existence, is the characteristic of sin. In the kingdom of the saints, however, all will be harmonious; there will be

> One kingdom, joy and union without end.

Before we can proceed to a final exposition of Milton's ethical purpose in the portrayal of Satan, we must

[31] Cf. *Paradise Lost,* V, 853–66.

understand exactly how union is broken and what law is denied when sin is committed. God, as we have already seen, is the fundamental law of the universe and is reflected in human conscience or reason. As a matter of fact, God is to be considered practically identical with reason. We learn this especially from Milton's proof of God's existence, which is explained in the *Christian Doctrine*, and to which we have already referred.[32] God is the force of conscience in the human soul, a law which makes itself felt in every finite mind. This idea is repeated again and again. When man fell, he forfeited his liberty and his reason simultaneously:

> Since thy original lapse, true Libertie
> Is lost, which alwayes with *right Reason* dwells,
> Twinn'd, and from her hath no dividual being.

The following are typical quotations from Milton. Before the Fall, Eve could say,

> We live
> Law to our selves; our Reason is our Law.

Sin consists in doing anything contrary to the innate reason, which "is free, and Reason he made right." Lawless and irrational passion is what man should avoid:

> Take heed lest Passion sway
> Thy Judgement to do aught which else free Will
> Would not admit.

[32] *P. W.*, IV, 15. Cf. above, p. 151. This fact is further indicated by the way in which Milton disproves the existence of the orthodox Trinity; cf. *P. W.*, IV, 95. Any conception not comprehensible by the human reason must be absurd.

Sin, then, consists in allowing passion to rule the reason.[33] This misrule is the same whether in the universe as a whole or in the finite creature; it constitutes the separation, the breaking of unity, of the finite from the infinite; and, because it takes from man the source of his reality, *it brings about the retrogression of the finite being to chaos*. This, as I understand it, is the great teaching of *Paradise Lost*.

Satan was an excellent, admirable, and glorious creature, but only a creature. He was a powerful reasoner; but there was one great flaw in his ratiocination: he thought he could defy the fundamental law of all existence. And he thought this because he considered his own being self-begotten. His mistake consisted in failing to recognize that he was but a portion of God, and that his glory and greatness depended upon staying close to and tending still nearer toward him. At the beginning of *Paradise Lost*, he was near the summit of creation; but, as he proceeded in his evil course, he descended in the direction of chaos, finding his only consolation in dragging others down with him into his own inevitable ruin.

Herein consists the moral tragedy: Satan not only recognizes his progressive degradation and increasing misery; he not only knows that—urged by his subjective constitution—he must commit evil to satisfy the evil within him;[34] but he also knows that all the injury he does to others will continue to redound with redou-

[33] This fact Denis Saurat was, I think, the first to point out.

[34] *Ibid.*, IX, 119–34.

bled fury upon his own devoted head, to make him unutterably miserable, and to render his torture progressively more and more exquisite and excruciating. He is the most tragic figure in literature. Unlike mortals in despair, he cannot hope for the cessation of his anguish. His portrayal is perfect, considered either as a treatise in ethics or as a work of art: and is not, after all, the sublimest tragedy artistic in proportion as it is ethical?

Milton's general moral teaching in *Paradise Lost*, then, is this: Reason, which is God's law in the cosmos and in the mind of man, must be observed. To observe it is to live in harmony with God; to trample it under foot is to separate ourselves from God and to break the cosmic unity. Lucifer—the great, the glorious, the elevated, the superb, the chief of the archangels—having despised the law by which the whole universe subsists as an organized and unified entity, having broken the unity of God, and having separated himself from the source of his reality, undergoes an unparalleled disintegration. Could Satan have established himself in the position which he tried to assume at the chronological beginning of *Paradise Lost*,[35] the whole order of things must have gone to wrack and ruin; chaos in the all would have ensued. The fundamental law of the whole universe would have to be thrown aside before he could be enthroned. In spite of his greatness, compared with men, Satan was—both figurately and literally—but a mathematical point in comparison with God. There is no

[35] Cf. *Paradise Lost*, V, 582.

struggle; but the archangel—in spite of some admirable protests at the beginning of *Paradise Lost,* indicative of the glory and greatness which he destroyed for himself by his own revolt—gradually withers into almost sheer nothingness.

What, finally, is the particular ethical teaching conveyed in the portrayal of Satan? I conceive it to be this: If Satan, who was so greatly superior to man in degree, but so like him in kind, was so utterly unsuccessful in his attempt to deny the validity of God's law—Reason—in the universe; if the misrule and anarchy of passion produced such fearful consequences in him, what will be the result when man, in his tiny way, attempts to do the same sort of thing that Satan tried? Man, the immeasurably weaker vessel, must be even more careful than the angels to maintain his harmony with God, the cosmos, the all-pervading and all-embracing unity. This is the way of God with men. We must obey the dictates of our conscience. This is Milton's philosophic and rationalistic religion: we must achieve harmony both with God and with our fellow-creatures, ascend toward the creator and complete spirituality, and become one with the infinite excellence.

There is no hero in *Paradise Lost.* Milton was not interested in heroes, human or divine. He was absorbed in the metaphysical and ethical problem of good and evil. The solution of that problem he has given us in its entirety by showing us Satan, the cosmic, though finite, power. To grasp the message of *Paradise Lost,* we need but realize the solution of the ethical problem of the Archfiend and apply it to ourselves. Milton's ethics become identical with his religion; and thus he

> assert[s] Eternal Providence,
> And justifie[s] the wayes of God to men.

We need not apologize for calling the message of *Paradise Lost* "modern." That it is in close affinity with the speeches of Browning's dying Paracelsus is obvious enough. Milton's solution of human happiness marks him a kindred spirit both with Guatama and with the author of the *Leaves of Grass. Paradise Lost* is a plea for a realization of the homogeneity and interdependence of all mankind and nature; the knowledge of such a status inculcates a desire for unity and brotherhood among the peoples of the earth and among the units of each social organization; it makes us all see that the good of the individual and that of society at large are one and the same. Lastly, it causes us to realize the universal potential equality of all existence: nothing is better or worse than anything else, except in degree. And this is the philosophy of social organization and these are the metaphysics which many advanced minds are proclaiming today. We cannot but feel that Whitman might have addressed the following to Milton as well as to the Crucified One:

> We saturate time and eras, that the
> men and women of races, ages to
> come, may prove brethren and lov-
> ers as we are.

CHAPTER VI

MILTON'S PERMANENT CONTRIBUTION TO THOUGHT AND CULTURE

The great bulk of criticism which has grown up about Milton regards him as a mere "poet"—the master of an eloquent and rhythmic diction and the possessor of a vast and daring imagination. Undoubtedly, it is true that he has appealed rather to the imagination than to the intellect; nevertheless, to compare the thought-content of his poetry with that of Keats, Shelley, or Swinburne would be absurd, for, first of all, Milton was interested in solving the basic problems of life, and with these he had had poignant experience. As Arnold has pointed out, Milton's poetry is simple, natural, and majestic to an extent attained by only two or three other poets in European history. And these qualities of style are but reflected qualities of thought.

One may read *Paradise Lost* with some profit and enjoyment without any knowledge of what lies behind it; but only a man well versed in the material which forms its content can appreciate it fully. The point is that to read Milton is not a mere trick, as reading Browning very largely is; Browning looks difficult, but is so only externally; Milton, however, is profound by reason of what his words imply. Milton has unusual simplicity and depth; to understand him one must have a general grasp of all his great doctrines and all the philosophies which influenced him. His poetry, however, is as clear as any containing simple but great conceptions can be. We ought, consequently, to reckon with his *ideas*.

Everything that he ever wrote, whether in prose or verse, has the remarkable distinction of being sane, profound, and fundamental. To what extent he has permeated the great minds of the English race since, it is now impossible to tell accurately; that he has done so more than any other English author with the possible exception of Shakespeare is established by such a vast and careful work as that of R. D. Havens.[1] He has shown the verbal reminiscences of Milton in English poetry; the intellectual influence cannot have been less; and the whole field of prose remains to be considered. What I mean to imply is that Milton's great conceptions have certainly not been without their effect. He has found fit audience, nor have they been so very few. He has influenced those who have been most influential; and his thinking is one of the inalienable inheritances of the English-speaking peoples.[2]

Milton thought much and vigorously about those great human problems concerning which the unthinking multitude believe they have definitive knowledge because they have been taught by dogmatic authority.

[1] *Influence of Milton on English Poetry.*

[2] Milton scholarship since 1918 has taken a turn which has increasingly recognized this fact.

These are the problems of religion, of government, and of morality. And Milton was, like Socrates, revolutionary and modern: this is simply saying that posterity has indorsed his views and repudiated those of his contemporaries.

Milton's influence in religion has been not only very great but also unique. Especially during the eighteenth century, *Paradise Lost* was exceedingly popular; it went through approximately a hundred editions in as many years; it lay on the table of almost every English family, along with the Bible. Anne Bradstreet knew Milton's poems very well; and such other American authors as Freneau and Trumbull reflect his influence both in detail and at large. Emerson had absorbed Milton almost as thoroughly as he had imbibed Plato. And to study the rise of the so-called English romantic poetry during the eighteenth century is largely to comprehend the vast influence of Spenser and Milton. But even the neo-classicists were under Milton's wizard spell: Addison affected his style; Pope praised his language, and his own poetry is studded with Miltonic phraseology. That a great religious poet, read so widely and so intensively by all intelligent people, should have been without religious influence is impossible. He has been accused of perpetuating the Christian myth; as Shelley said, he stamped that myth with the mark of genius. What we must realize, however, is the vast influence Milton exerted in modifying the general conception of religion. He transferred it from the field of dogma and placed it in the domain of loveliness. What was harsh or irrational, he made kind and comprehensible. What had before appealed to man's sense of sin, now came to appeal to his sense of beauty. Milton would, he hoped, "leave something so written to aftertimes, as they should not willingly let it die"; and he would "teach . . . . over the whole book of sanctity and virtue." Of that religion which was before but a cruel and rugged creed, bequeathed by the past to crush the present and the future, and supported by bigotry, persecution, and asceticism, he made an image of such supernal majesty, interpreted in the light of Greek and Renaissance philosophy, that it has been capable of thrilling both the minds and the imaginations of a great posterity. The myth which had been a vehicle of terror he made a vehicle of beauty. There can be no doubt that Milton's influence has been very extensive in softening and intellectualizing religious conceptions; that men have obtained from *Paradise Lost* and *Paradise Regained* what could never have been had from sermons and treatises on theology. Milton has influenced Christianity from within, but the effect has been much the same as that of hostile rationalism. In effect, he has done much to destroy the horrible rigor of a tyrannical dogma by a change in emphasis, by drawing attention away from the concrete and practical toward the imaginative.

Milton's influence in the evolution of religion which has occurred during the last two centuries and a half is, then, probably far greater than is usually thought. He approached Christianity not only with respect and reverence but, during his later years, with a strong personal need for its consolation. Yet he absorbed its philosophy with an attitude of mind which enabled him to find in the Bible what others did *not* find there. He could accept nothing in Christianity as he found it. Even while changing all its main features, however, he retained its essential teachings. He appears, therefore, as an orthodox Christian; but he made his religion a persuasive force, not a compulsive one, as it always has been with the dogmatists. He appealed to his reader's intellectual, moral, and aesthetic nature and to his desire for perfection and harmony with God. He did not preach the terrors of the law or emphasize human depravity; nor did he appeal to an ignorant fear.

We can scarcely overestimate Milton's influence in humanizing medieval Christianity. Especially in the pamphlets, he demanded such religious reforms as are compatible with modern thought. He set his face absolutely against a state church, against any sort of compulsion in religious matters, and against tithes or any kind of involuntary contributions to support an ecclesiastical institution. He maintained that religion must work by persuasion only, must "govern the inner man," must never resort to force. All religious opinions must be tolerated equally. No extensive education is necessary in religion, even for ministers; neither regular churches

nor a professional clergy should be maintained.[3] Not
doctrine, but charity should be made fundamental:

> Onely add
> Deeds to thy knowledge answerable; add Faith;
> Add Vertue, Patience, Temperance; add Love
> By name to come call'd Charitie, the soul
> Of all the rest.

And in his major poems, his great subjective revelation,
Milton emphasizes the grandeur and mercy of God, the
necessity of rational law, the fundamental goodness of
man, and the glorious destiny he may achieve by the
power of his will.

The influence of Milton's political theories, being
more explicit than his religious, must have been no less.
Those theories are the direct forerunners of Rousseau,
the French Revolution, and the Constitution of the United States. It is true that Milton did not announce them
for the first time; but it is also true that he brought
them to the attention of more people than any other
thinker down to Rousseau; and he did what the French-
man did not: he applied them to a great and particular
crisis in human affairs, and made them the basis for justifying an wholly unprecedented political action.

Milton's theory that all men are born free, that all
government is delegated, that power always remains in
the body-politic, and that all governors are responsible

[3] Of course, as J. M. Robertson has pointed out, in *A Short History of Christianity*, such reforms would soon cause the disappearance
of any religion in a short time.

to the governed only but to them wholly were extraordinary opinions among Englishmen in 1648. The Episcopal church had one theory, the result of its regal origin, on which it prided itself more than on any other: and this was the absolute obedience of subjects to their king.[4] And, as the event proved, the Presbyterians were little behind the Episcopalians in offering abject obeisance to royalty. Later, during the reign of Charles II, Sir Robert Filmer expounded in full the theory of the divine right of kings. He argued that all men are born slaves, and that it is impious for them to try to throw off their natural yoke. He taught that no matter what the king might do, subjects might never rebel, or even protest; even if he should take away both their possessions and their lives, they had no ground for considering themselves injured. These doctrines became the rallying point of the High Church; and even three years of outrageous tyranny by James II, combined with his attack on episcopacy itself, was insufficient to efface from the minds of most of the bishops or the majority of the English people this doctrine of "non-resistance." Such a theory as Filmer's, of course, would now be a public joke; but in 1687 it was a matter of life and death.

Milton's political theories are those on which all modern liberal governments are based; perhaps the best way to present his doctrine and conclude the present

[4] Milton seems to defend this very theory in a tract of 1643. But this was before he was interested in politics and before they presented any vital issue to him.

topic is to quote a few passages from his *Tenure of Kings and Magistrates:*

No man, who knows aught, can be so stupid to deny, that all men naturally were born free, being the image and resemblance of God himself, and were, by privilege above all the creatures, born to command, and not to obey: and that they lived so, till from the root of Adam's transgression falling among themselves to do wrong and violence, and foreseeing that such courses must needs tend to the destruction of them all, they agreed by common league to bind each other from mutual injury, and jointly to defend themselves against any that gave disturbance or opposition to such agreement. Hence came cities, towns, and commonwealths. And because no faith in all was found sufficiently binding, they saw it needful to ordain some authority that might restrain by force and punishment what was violated against peace and common right.

This authority and power of self-defense and preservation being originally and naturally in every one of them, and unitedly in them all; for ease, for order, and lest each man should be his own partial judge, they communicated and derived either to one, whom for the eminence of his wisdom and integrity they chose above the rest, or to more than one, whom they thought of equal deserving; the first was called a king; the other, magistrates; not to be their lords and masters . . . ., but to be their deputies and commissioners, to execute, by the bond of their intrusted power, that justice, which else every man by the bond of nature and of covenant must have executed for himself, and for one another. And to him that shall consider well, why among free persons one man by civil right should bear authority and jurisdiction over another, no other end or reason can be imaginable.

These for a while governed well, and with much equity decided all things at their own arbitrement; till the temptation of such a power, left absolute in their hands, perverted them at length to injustice and partiality. Then did they, who now by trial had found the danger and inconveniences of committing arbitrary power to any, invent laws, either framed or consented to by all, that should confine and limit the authority of whom they chose to govern them: that any man, of whose failing they had proof, might no more rule over them, but law and reason, abstracted as much as might be from personal errors and frailties. "While, as the magistrate was set above the people, so the law was set above the magistrate." When this would not serve, but that the law was either not executed, or misapplied, they were constrained from that time, the only remedy left them, to put conditions and take oaths from all kings and magistrates at their first instalment, to do impartial justice by law: who, upon those terms and no other, received allegiance from the people, that is to say, bond or covenant to obey them in execution of those laws, which they, the people, had themselves made or assented to. And this ofttimes with express warning, that if the king or magistrate proved unfaithful to his trust, the people would be disengaged. . . . .

. . . . The power of kings and magistrates is nothing else but what is derivative, transferred, and commited to them in trust from the people to the common good of them all, in whom the power yet remains fundamentally, and cannot be taken from them, without a violation of their natural birthright. . . . .

. . . . To say, as is usual, the king hath as good right to his crown and dignity as any man to his inheritance, is to make the subject no better than the king's slave, his chattel, or his possession that may be bought or sold. . . . . Unless the people must be thought created all for him, he not for them, and they all in one body inferior to him single; which were a kind of treason against the dignity of mankind to affirm.

A king, says Milton, may see among his subjects

many thousand men for wisdom, virtue, nobleness of mind, and all other respects but the fortune of his dignity, far above him.

Thus the argument is concluded:

It follows, lastly, that since the king or magistrate holds his authority of the people, both originally and naturally for their good, in the first place, and not his own, then may the people, as oft as they shall judge it for the best, either choose him or reject him, retain him or depose him, though no tyrant, merely by the liberty and right of freeborn men to be governed as seems to them best.

A tyrant [is] . . . . the common enemy, against whom what the people may lawfully do, as against a common pest and destroyer of mankind, I suppose no man of clear judgment need go further to be guided than by the very principles of nature in him.

This whole theory, it is easy to see, is both practical and speculative and solely rational; Milton goes on to invoke every historical fact in favor of his theory and every biblical text that can possibly be made to do duty. But, after all, it is clear that his doctrine depends upon his conviction that all men, as he says, are naturally born free, which is very much the same thing as saying that all men are created equal. How modern is this!

But in no field of human interest has Milton proved more radical, more prophetic, and probably more influential than in the domestic. His *Doctrine and Discipline of Divorce,* has, by some, been pronounced his greatest work in prose. It is certain that he said emphatically what had never been emphasized before; that he maintained a most revolutionary and individualistic point of view; that he was most severely condemned for this by his contemporaries; that he enforced his argument with every principle favorable to divorce known even yet; and that all development in domestic theory during the last two hundred years has been in the direction of his thesis. It is true that he idealized marriage too much and that he assumed too heavily on the merits of ordinary people; it is true that he tended to disregard the practical problems which necessarily make it a more or less sordid institution. Nevertheless, after all concessions have been made, it is certain that Milton formulated and promulgated a great theory of sex-relationships which is perhaps destined to revolutionize social organization. Just as, in political theory, Milton is the direct forerunner of Rousseau, Paine, and Jefferson, so, in the domestic field, he is the direct antecedent of Godwin, Shelley, Meredith, Whitman, Shaw, and Edward Carpenter. The present divorce laws in Soviet Russia are a practical realization of Milton's teaching on the subject.

That Milton's first divorce pamphlet was the result of a sharp experience and the outburst of a man who had been ignorant concerning women must be evident enough. The thirty-five-year-old scholar, poet, and philosopher probably expected to find his exalted ideal of womanhood, reared by a poetic imagination and fed by a great intellect, fulfilled in poor little seventeen-year-old Mary Powell. The result was, of course, disastrous; she undoubtedly had no desire to meet his needs, and she must have been even less able to do so. The ignorant and helpless wife was probably terrified by the serious thinker and controversialist who demanded that his wife

be a "help meet for him." This was a fearful experience
—something wholly new in Milton's life. It brought him
face to face with actuality; his puerile theories were forgotten. He found that women had plenty of flesh and
blood, and that marriage was a most serious undertaking. Out of the shock and stress of this experience, he
framed a doctrine that he thought would largely elim-
inate the evils of private life; and without in any way
alluding to his own miseries he dealt with general principles universally applicable.

According to his usual method of procedure in controversy, Milton left the merely practical considerations
largely out of sight (which he probably thought would
adjust themselves), and at once attacked the whole established doctrine of sex-relationships. He maintained
that marriage is only a household contract, entered into
by two people at choice; and, like any other, to be broken likewise. With this institution, the chief object of
which is "solace of mind," the Church is in no way concerned; nor has the state any other function than to register marriages and divorces, and, in case there are children, see to it that the parents provide for them. Milton
argued that if both parties desire divorce, the law has no
right to prevent it; as a matter of fact, law courts have
no business to bandy up and down the private disaffec-
tions of wedlock. If the husband alone desires divorce,
he is either just in his demand and so ought to be granted it; or else he is unjust, and no wife will desire to live
with such a man. The law can have no function except

in arranging matters of property; it cannot judge of the "rooted antipathies of nature." Private divorce, then, by mutual consent, or by the will of the aggrieved party, must become a recognized principle.[5] This is Milton's fundamental thesis; now let us glance for a few moments at its constituent elements.

Milton's method of argument is largely that of his day; but his attitude is diametrically opposed to it. Seemingly, his chief problems were reconciling the words of Christ in regard to divorce and those of Moses on the same subject, and finding a definition for "fornication"[6] suitable to his needs. The whole treatise is filled with appeal to precedent and authority, and the scriptures are regarded as final. But it is obvious throughout that this dependence is but a thin veil to cover a most radical and revolutionary doctrine; whatever agrees with Milton is excellent; whatever disagrees with him is absurd or ridiculous. For example, the "burning" of which Paul speaks must be desire for intellectual communion; the "natural uncleanness" for which Moses allows divorce must be contrariety of mind. That the Gospel should be more cruel than the Mosaic law is unthinkable. It is amusing to see Milton wrench his authorities; but in this very act the basic man, rationalistic and individualistic,

[5] Cf. *P. W.*, III, 263-68.

[6] It is sufficiently interesting to notice that in 1642 Milton accepted "fornication" in its usual significance; cf. *P. W.*, III, 122. Incidentally, this proves that the *Christian Doctrine* was written after 1644, for in that document we find the new definition of the word. Cf. above, pp. 161-62.

steps forth with almost ineffable courage and independence. His reason was the only infallible authority that Milton knew.

The whole *Doctrine and Discipline* is redolent of personal experience; frequent passages of unmatchable poignancy punctuate it like howls of agony, to which a poet only could have given utterance. A man needs "an intimate and speaking help, a ready and reviving associate"; he must not be burdened with "a mute and spiritless mate," "an uncomplying discord of nature . . . ., an image of earth and phlegm." He despised "the empty husk of an outside matrimony," and he refused "to grind in the mill of an undelightful and servile copulation." A man unfortunately married has been "trained up by a deceitful bait into a snare of misery" "to remedy a sublunary and bestial burning," with "an accidental companion of propagation." "Instead of being one flesh, these will be rather two carcasses chained unnaturally together; or, as it may happen, a living soul coupled to a dead corpse."[7] To prohibit divorce, he says, is the doctrine of devils no less than the forbidding to marry. We cannot bind "the irreducible antipathies of nature," "the disunions of complaining nature in chains together" "to be cooped up . . . . in a mockery of wedlock." "To couple hatred, therefore, though wedlock try all her

[7] It was these passages that especially appealed to Farquhar, who copied them and several others into his *Beaux' Stratagem*. Cf. the author's "Influence of Milton's Divorce Tracts on Farquhar's *Beaux' Stratagem*," *Publications of the Modern Language Association*, March, 1924.

golden links, and borrow to her aid all the iron manacles and fetters of the law, it does but seek to twist a rope of sand."[7] Although Milton proudly affirmed that he was engaged "in [a] general labour of reformation," the personal note in his first divorce tract is not to be mistaken.

To suppose that Milton to any extent advocated divorce because of a strain of moral laxness in him is of course absurd. It is generally admitted that no other English author—not even Spenser[8]—(and the English are noted for strictness in morality) can compare with Milton in moral purity and elevation. He defends himself nobly in the *Apology for Smectymnuus* against all imputation of lewdness. The truth is that Milton would not do what the majority of mankind do with little scruple; he would not transgress a law against which he did not register an emphatic protest and the justice of which he did not publicly impugn. His code of ethics was such that when he took the vows of matrimony he would either observe those vows or publish to the world his reasons for not doing so. In fact, his was exactly the kind of mind which will demand for others legal rights which he will not take illegally for himself. He rebelled against social rules which, he thought, are not based upon the moral law but upon the fabrication of tyrannical bigotry. He realized very clearly that priests made marriage a sacrament to increase their temporal power.[9] He

[8] Cf. story of the Squyre of Dames, *Faerie Queene*, Book III.

[9] Cf. *P. W.*, III, 22. This passage is confirmed by many others of the same nature.

felt keenly the need of that intimate intellectual and sympathetic companionship which can exist only between the sexes; if marriage gives, not this, but unutterable misery instead, it must be dissolved and the parties permitted to seek more fortunate alliances. And those chiefly concerned must be the only judges of the issue. We have as signal a presentation of Milton's exalted ethics in his divorce tracts as in his *Comus*.

In composing the *Doctrine and Discipline,* Milton had, as it seems to me, a threefold purpose: first, to improve public morality; second, to relieve innumerable individuals from irremediable torment; and, third, to make marriage what it should be, "a mystery of joy." It was Milton's conviction that if those unhappily married are denied freedom "they suddenly break out into some wide rupture of open vice," and repair their misery as best they can by visiting the stews or by increasing general private immorality. He wishes

to restore this . . . . lost heritage [divorce], into the household state: wherewith be sure that peace and love, the best subsistence of a Christian family, will return home from whence they are now banished; places of prostitution will be less haunted, the neighbor's bed less attempted, the yoke of prudent and manly discipline will be generally submitted to; sober and well-ordered living will soon spring up in the commonwealth.

It is a historical fact that vice grows into a gangrene when some unnatural virtue is assumed.[10] And Milton says that we must "not be thus overcurious to strain at

[10] This is to be seen particularly in the church, which denied marriage to the priests.

atoms, and yet to stop every vent and cranny of permissive liberty." "Honest liberty is the greatest foe to license." The inviolability of marriage has brought with it, thought Milton, many moral evils, which he sought to remedy. But his moral purpose was undoubtedly less significant than his individualism. Above all else he pitied "the pining of a sad spirit wedded to loneliness." Looking about him he saw thousands grinding in the mill of a desolate and disconsolate wedlock; their lives were burdens to them, and their thoughts turned naturally to atheism and the subversion of the government. Any system of things, Milton assumes, that places unendurable evils upon individuals for no fault of their own is not worthy of preservation. The land, the laws, and society exist for the benefit of the individuals who constitute the community; and their interests are of paramount importance. Milton's third and greatest purpose was to make marriage the institution it should be: the most harmonious and sympathetic of human relationships; an intellectual union so complete that nothing could be added to enhance its perfection. The wife and husband ought to live in intimate intellectual communion; when they do not, there is no actual marriage.

Milton's ideal is too high to be realized by the human race as it now is, but it is an exalted goal toward which to strive. He always emphasizes the intellectual, the spiritual sides, and minimizes the physical. When there is no union of mind, he says, "all corporal delight will soon become unsavoury and contemptible." "What

can be fouler incongruity, a greater violence to the re-
vered secret of nature, than to sow the sorrow of man's
nativity with the seed of two incoherent and incombin-
ing dispositions?" "I suppose it will be allowed us that
marriage is a human society, and that all human society
must proceed from the mind rather than the body."
Those who marry because of physical desire Milton refers to as "such cattle." This ideal is the essence of the
Doctrine and Discipline of Divorce.

What, then, constitutes a true marriage? This can
best be answered in Milton's own words:

> When is it that God may be said to join? when the parties
> and their friends consent? No, surely; for that may concur to the
> lewdest ends. Or is it when church rites are finished? Neither;
> for the efficacy of those depends upon the presupposed fitness of
> either party. Perhaps after carnal knowledge. Least of all; for
> that may join persons whom neither law nor nature dares join.
> It is left, that only then when the minds are fitly disposed and
> enabled to maintain a cheerful conversation, to the solace and love
> of each other, according as God intended and promised in the very
> first foundation of matrimony, "I will make him a help-meet for
> him;" for surely what God intended and promised, that only can
> be thought to be joining, and not the contrary.

Because he elevated the necessity of intellectual
union and spiritual harmony so much, it is not strange
that Milton's basis for divorce is of a related nature.
The mind, he says, takes precedence over the body.
Neither adultery nor natural frigidity are grievances
in any way comparable with incompatability of mind.
"Natural hatred," he says, "wherever it arises, is a

greater evil in marriage than the accident of adultery, a greater defrauding, a greater injustice, yet not blamable." Adultery, he continues, is "but a transient injury, and soon amended, I mean as to the party against whom the trespass is: but that other [is] an unspeakable and unremitting sorrow and offence, whereof no amends can be made, no cure, no ceasing but by divorce, which, like a divine touch in one moment heals all, and in one instant hushes outrageous tempests into a sudden stillness and peaceful calm." Incompatability of mind, he avers, consists of "those natural and perpetual hinderances of society . . . ., which cannot be removed; for [as] such as they are aptest to cause an unchangeable offence, so are they not capable of reconcilement, because not of amendment; they do not break indeed, but they annihilate the bands of marriage more than adultery."

Consequently, as marriage consists not in the union of bodies but in the union of minds, no marriage ever exists without intellectual unity. If there is neither solace nor peace in the sexual union, such a joining is automatically abrogated. "When it shall be found by their apparent unfitness that their continuing to be man and wife is against the glory of God and their mutual happiness, it may assure them that God never joined them." To consider such a marriage lawful is to "canonize it as a tyraness . . . . over the enfranchised life and soul of man." "Such a marriage can be no marriage."

The misery of an unfortunate wedlock caused by the helpless and irremediable discord of jarring natures is a subject upon which Milton expatiates endlessly. The prohibition of divorce "hath changed the blessing of matrimony not seldom into a familiar and coinhabiting mischief; at least into a drooping and disconsolate household captivity, without refuge or redemption." Too frequently those who enter into it become "the bondmen of a luckless and helpless matrimony."

No place in heaven or earth, except hell, where charity may not enter: yet marriage, the ordinance of our solace and contentment, the remedy of our loneliness, will not admit now either of charity or mercy, to come in and mediate, or pacify the fierceness of this gentle ordinance, the unremedied loneliness of this remedy. . . . . He who marries, intends as little to conspire his own ruin, as he that swears allegiance.

No effect of tyranny can sit more heavy on the commonwealth than this household unhappiness on the family. And farewell all hope of true reformation in the state, while such an evil as this lies undiscerned or unregarded in the house: on the redress whereof depends not only the spiritful and orderly life of our grown men, but the willing and careful education of our children.

Now, if any two be but once handed in the church, and have tasted in any sort the nuptial bed, let them find themselves never so mistaken in their dispositions through any error, concealment, or misadventure, that through their different tempers, thoughts, and constitutions, they can neither be to one another a remedy against loneliness, nor live in any union or contentment all their days; yet they shall, so they be but found suitably weaponed to the least possibility of sensual enjoyment, be made, spite of antipathy, to fadge together, and combine as they may to their unspeakable weariness, and despair of all sociable delight in the ordinance which God established to that very end.

The solitariness of man . . . . lies under a worse condition than the loneliest single life; for in single life the absence and remoteness of a helper might inure him to expect his own comforts out of himself, or to seek with hope; but here the continual sight of his deluded thoughts, without cure, must needs be to him, if especially his complexion incline him to melancholy, a daily trouble and pain of loss, in some degree like that which reprobates feel.

A bad marriage

hath drawn together, in two persons ill embarked in wedlock, the sleeping discords and enmities of nature, lulled on purpose with some false bait, that they may wake to agony and strife, later than prevention could have wished; if from the bent of just and honest intentions beginning what was begun and so continuing, all that is equal, all that is fair and possible hath been tried, and no accommodation likely to succeed; what folly is it still to stand combatting and battering against invincible causes and effects, with evil upon evil, till either the best of our days be lingered out, or ended with some speeding sorrow!

Such degrading servitude it can be the duty of no human being to sustain.

When therefore an individual finds himself "bound fast to uncomplying discord of nature," "an image of earth and phlegm," "a thorn intestine," "a cleaving mischief," it is both his right and his duty to separate himself completely from such a one. From all the foregoing, Milton's great proposition follows inevitably:

"That indisposition, unfitness, or contrariety of mind, arising from a cause in nature unchangeable, hindering and ever likely to hinder the main benefits of conjugal society, which are solace and peace; is a greater reason of divorce than natural frigidity, especially if there be no children, and that there be mutual consent."

It is impossible, says Milton, that God "should bind against a prime and principal scope of his own institu-

tion, or engage a blameless creature to his perpetual sorrow." And this universal right to divorce is a private
matter:

> The radical and innocent affections of nature . . . . is not
> within the diocese of the law to tamper with. . . . . But because
> this is such a secret kind of fraud or theft, as cannot be discov-
> ered by law . . . . therefore to divorce was never counted a po-
> litical or civil offence. . . . . The law can only appoint the just
> and equal conditions of divorce. . . . . God . . . . [did not] au-
> thorize a judicial court to toss about and divulge the unaccount-
> able and secret reason of disaffection between man and wife, as a
> thing most improperly answerable to any such kind of trial.

The need for divorce, as Milton explains at length,
can never be removed by greater deliberation before
marriage. As he realized, if either party may be a gainer
by an inviolable contract, it will be to his advantage to
deceive the other before its consummation. If divorce is
freely permitted, there can be little object in pre-marital
hypocrisy; it will be to the advantage of prospective
brides or grooms to exhibit themselves as they actually
are. Furthermore, it is precisely those studious, sincere,
and most virtuous people who usually are most unfortunate in their first marriage choice; because, being without experience and having developed an ideal of their
own, they are easily deceived by a designing person. On
the other hand, men who are fickle and who have little
respect for sexual morality are most fortunate in their
matches; for every experience with women has given to

them the wisdom to be gained from a marriage solemnized by the Church and the State.

At this point we ought, perhaps, say a word concerning the relations between Milton's metaphysics and his doctrine of divorce. According to the Western Fathers of the fourth and fifth centuries, marriage was an absolute evil, because it was a pandering to the indwelling human devil, the flesh. The church came to permit marriage only under the severest strictures, making it a sacrament and caring not at all for its intellectual aspect but considering only its carnal. According to Milton's metaphysics, man is composed of dichotomous matter and spirit, which, being both of God, are divine, but of which mind or spirit is the higher aspect. It follows therefore naturally that Milton should regard the intellectual union as the essential one, and the carnal as subservient and practically indifferent. Thus, adultery, which the canon law regarded as so extremely heinous, Milton regarded as of little significance. The acts of the body are not evil—they are simply unimportant. There is nothing contaminating in new sexual unions provided the intellectual sympathy precede. But the physical union without the deep unity and sympathy of mind which it presupposes is the most horrible immorality. Thus children born in wedlock of parents who do not really love each other are, Milton says, by no means better than those born wholly without the bonds of matrimony.

The consequences of Milton's domestic theory are indeed far-reaching. For more than two centuries after it was published practically no attention was paid to it. In his own day he was regarded with horror because of it, and was accused of being the founder of a sect of divorcists. It is only during the last thirty or forty years that any of Milton's ideals have begun to be realized. In England there is even yet no divorce on those grounds which Milton makes all-important; but in the more liberal United States another tale is being told. Although Milton does not accord wives and husbands equal powers of divorce,[11] such equality follows naturally from his theory when applied to modern life. In effect, Milton's theory may be called a qualified form of "free-love." But it does not remove the responsibility incurred by marriage; it does not in any way tend to cause promiscuity of sex-relationships—in fact, it would reduce it; and it makes the marital institution even more essential to human happiness than it could be under any other theory. It removes completely any stigma that may now be attached to the breaking of its bond. Under Milton's system, the present marriage contract would have to be remodeled completely. All feeling of compulsion would cease. The sense of a physical ownership of each other which husbands and wives now so often feel to be proper would of course be abolished. Furthermore, marriage would become far less commercialized than it now is—it would almost cease to be an institution of property. And, far more important than this, both parties to the union

[11] As both C. L. Powell and A. H. Gilbert have maintained. But I cannot agree with them.

would know that the continuance of it must depend upon giving satisfaction to the other; and this would cause a totally different policy on the part of millions of people from what we find now.

I take the *Doctrine and Discipline of Divorce* to be Milton's most fundamental and far-reaching contribution to thought. It is not only ultra-modern, but it is something yet unrealized, although perhaps to be achieved.

It is unreasonable to doubt that Milton's distinctly intellectual influence has been great. The rationalism and individualism, of which we have said so much and which constitute the very essence of his thought, have made themselves felt very extensively. His prose works have gone through about a dozen complete editions in two hundred years, and many selections from them have been distributed everywhere. His *Areopagitica* and tractate "Of Education" are universally known. His everlasting insistence upon the majesty of the human mind and its intrinsic powers has helped to form the convictions of thousands of thinking men. The effect of reading his work is that one's desire for knowledge is intensified, that one's self-reliance is increased, and that one begins to have a modern instead of a medieval conception of life as a whole, if one did not have it before. And most people did not until the middle of the nineteenth century.

Only a single topic remains to be considered. We cannot well doubt the influence of Milton's prose; but it was in his poetry that he made his largest contribution. So much has been written about this that it is indeed difficult to add anything; but statements of appreciation are subjective and personal, and may, therefore, be infinitely various.

Much of the power in Milton's poetry is due directly to his character; we might expect this in such highly subjective writing as his. He is one of the few men in our literature whose life was one great and practical action fought through in the arena of national affairs; whose principles and labors, like Shelley's, were neither theoretical nor ineffectual; whose actions and motives remain, under the strictest scrutiny, far above reproach; who never did anything except for a most elevated purpose; whose sole dominating passion was to make the human race better and so happier; who was as wholly emancipated from his past as Whitman was from his; and who seems to have cared very little or not at all for mere material wealth. Every pamphlet and poem, from the first to the last, is inspired by the central Miltonic ideal of purity, excellence, self-dependence, and power;[12] and this it is which constitutes the mainspring of Milton's character.

Milton's poetry is endowed with a half-score of qualities which one seeks in vain to parallel in other English

[12] Perhaps this statement does not hold true with regard to *Samson Agonistes*.

poetry and which render his work unique for its kind of excellence. It seems to me that the first of these qualities is mastery of language. For this many critics have praised him beyond all praise. He is "the mighty-mouthed inventor of harmonies," but he is also the author of the exquisite "L'Allegro" and "Il Penseroso." He understood and could play upon the whole gamut of expression, from the smallest to the greatest, always composing in such a way as never to be equaled by any other on the instrument which he employed. From the many-sounding chimes of "L'Allegro" to the powerful orchestration of *Paradise Lost* and *Samson Agonistes* a great interval exists; yet their author could employ the most suitable and imperishable language of which we can conceive to express every mood, thought, or feeling. Coleridge said that Milton's poetry is put together in such a way that it recites itself; if we but change a single syllable or misplace a single accent in it, the charm of the whole is destroyed. And it is certainly true, as anyone who has memorized passages from Milton knows, that there is very little danger of making any mistake in repeating his lines. It is quite otherwise especially with Byron's early poetry, which was written rapidly, which exhibits little mastery of language, and which can be changed variously to suit the reciter. Milton's poetry came forth in its perfect and final estate. Mark Pattison called "Lycidas" the high-water mark of English poetry.

The profound and various melodies of Milton's verse

are without parallel in our literature. The note struck in the "Ode on the Morning of Christ's Nativity" was but a feeble prelude to "Lycidas" and *Paradise Lost*. The elegy on the death of King, with its recurring minor and major musical strains, is as much a tone-poem as "Finlandia." In the great-epic, the music is incomprehensibly subtle and profound. Milton dispenses with all artificial aids, such as rhyme and stanzaic forms, and relies wholly upon his sheer genius. The rhythm wholly transcends the limits of foot, of line, and even of paragraph. Every book of *Paradise Lost* is a unit and its rhythm cannot be sensed adequately if read in portions. One rhythm running through four or five lines, seems with incalculable variations, to repeat that of the preceding and succeeding portions; and these in turn, wheel within wheel, become factors in larger symphonic movements. The whole rises, sweeps, and undulates in ravishing melody, with many overtones, minors, and majors; there is infinite modulation and harmony. The effect of the whole is unforgettable, but totally beyond exposition. The tone-color of *Paradise Lost* is more gorgeous than the somber colorings of *Paradise Regained*. In *Samson,* Milton achieves the freest and most various melodies to be found in his poetry. In many passages we find ourselves on the borderline between harmony and discord; but the most poignant melody is precisely that in which we find a hint of clashing strains. All in all, as a master of profound and various harmonies, Milton is unequaled in English literature.

In the third place, Milton's poetry has a peculiar

value in its intense subjectivity and in the strength of the character it so faithfully reveals. As Coleridge and Taine both pointed out, the genius of Shakespeare is transfused throughout all the materials of his art so that the author is himself nowhere revealed; but Milton gathered everything up into himself and gave it a tinge characteristic of himself alone. Whenever we read a work of Milton, we are face to face with its author. Thus his writings possess to an extraordinary degree that quality which Newman says is peculiar to higher literature. And De Quincy singles out *Paradise Lost* as a supreme example of *literature of power*.

The very elevated ideals of Milton are peculiar to his thought. Among these ideals are uncompromising physical and intellectual purity; absolute superiority to all slavery to passion, superstition, or error; complete harmony with God and our fellow-men; and activity in life depending upon rationalistic and individualistic premises. These principles are coherent, simple, unified, and clearly expressed. They constitute a very important element of his message to the world and are inseparable from their author.

The fifth outstanding quality of Milton's poetry is unity; this it possesses taken as a whole as well as in individual poems. They possess unity of design, structure, thought, and impression: they do all they propose to accomplish, and contain nothing superfluous. The unity of *Paradise Lost* is especially wonderful; it is so in the large as well as in all the details. There is nothing contradictory in the whole poem; all the materials of the "vast design" are under the perfect control of the architect who is also the artificer. It is evident that Milton had thought through to the last detail every portion of the whole conception; and everything that enters into it is a necessary complement to every other portion. Nothing is repeated; nothing is left out; nothing is discordant or contradictory. Although the whole is exceedingly complex, every part is so well ordered that the entire design takes on an air of extreme simplicity. Into the construction of the poem enter metaphysics, theology, architecture, music, military theory, ethics, and a setting that constitutes the universe. But it seems as simple as a schoolboy's theme. The reason, of course, is that Milton was so thorough a master of his subject that to him it *was* simple; therefore, it seems so to us likewise. It possesses a spherical completeness.

The seriousness and depth of Milton's convictions are an integral part of his poetic achievement. From early youth he had meditated "an immortality of fame," and his conscious purpose of being an apostle to posterity is such as we find in perhaps no other man of letters. Throughout his works we find proud references to the high mission and purpose which he considered his by divine bestowal. The result of this feeling was that everything he undertook assumed an importance and high seriousness which are otherwhere unequaled.[13] Milton is

[13] See the opening pages of the *Defensio Secunda,* where he imagines himself as addressing at once all the *intellectuelles* of Europe and them as listening intently, almost in reverence and awe.

so enormously *sincere* in what he says; all human existence seems to depend on believing him and acting upon his teaching. This is the reason that he has been called cold and distant, that there is so little of the gay, the light, the humorous in him. When a man is settling the affairs of mankind, he is scarcely in a jesting mood. The depth of Miltonic conviction pervades every line he ever wrote.

In the *Reason of Church Government*, Milton declares that he will never deal with mere "verbal curiosities," but will teach solid wisdom. If ornament is superinduced decoration, Milton's poetry is nearly destitute of it. Everything in it is a part of the same thing; thought and word blend into perfect harmony, the one being the image and the echo of the other. The mythological allusion with which it is studded is as much a part of the poetry as the words in which it is couched. The simplicity of Milton is equaled only by Homer; the naked metal is immediately visible and consists of imperishable gold. There are no frills, no artificial aids; both thought and execution give evidence of a master who can depend for power upon genius solely and need not use the trickery of a meretricious art.

The eighth quality is majesty, the natural companion of simplicity. The virtue of Milton lies in his height and breadth rather than in his garb. He rises naturally to the higher levels of poesy, and sails on mighty and easy pinion. His dignity and grandeur are as natural to him as are its massiveness and loftiness to a mountain.

The source of Milton's majesty is his own soul, whence he drew a superabundant supply.

The word *Miltonic* is almost synonymous with sublimity. As defined by Burke, the "sublime" is that which inspires awe bordering on fear by means either of greatness (the extensive sublime) or of power (the dynamic sublime). Milton is a master of both. Unabashed, he explores the abyss, the horrors of hell, and the magnificence of heaven; he relates how the rising world of waters waste and wild were formed into a firm terraqueous globe; he portrays the wars of heaven, which surpass anything elsewhere imagined by a mortal; and he is no less sublime in his portrayal of Satan's moral world—that second universe which, upon contemplation, as Kant said, fills the mind with awe and wonder. "The poet blind yet bold" leaves no portion of the physical or moral world unexplored. And the language of *Paradise Lost*, which we find prefigured in "Lycidas," is always congruent with the conceptions it reveals and conveys. One cannot read Milton's poetry without experiencing an emotion which is partly admiration, partly awe, partly aspiration, and closely akin to a thrill of terror. And this is sublimity. A single line, which appealed vividly to the imagination of De Quincey, illustrates what I mean. Think of the power which visioned

the Gate
With dreadful Faces throng'd and fierie arms.

The last characteristic peculiarly Miltonic consists of his extraordinary conceptions. His early image of

Christ in the "Ode" was indicative of what he could do. Revealed in his poetry, being, in fact, the very woof of it, his conceptions are given to us clothed by a vast and daring imagination. Where else in literature will we find anything to compare with the Satan, the modal Trinity or cosmos, the chaos, the hell, the warring seraphim, and the terrestrial universe of *Paradise Lost?* Where else may we find such a profound exposition of the cosmic moral law, the relation between the finite and the infinite, and the unity of all existence as Milton has given us? Where else shall we look for an exposition of the larger life of man which embraces so universally all the major elements of human existence? Milton is unique in the greatness, the clarity, and the simplicity of his grand poetic conceptions.

The reading of Milton acts upon the sensitive reader like the playing of a great number of orchestras in infinite harmony; yet his *chief* appeal is to the intellect. He lifts us out of ourselves, and thrills us as no other force can do. He gives us a new and broader ideal to grasp; he elevates us to a feeling of brotherhood with God and man alike. He leaves no responding chord of the intellectual, moral, or aesthetic being untouched. He bears us on wings sublime up through the starry heavens and down through the nether deeps. Borne aloft by him on the wings of song, we seem to experience the fabled but far-famed music of the spheres.

INDEX

Abailard, 48

Absalom and Achitophel, 181, 200 n.

Absolute predestination, 24 n., 30, 32, 37, 45 n., 53, 54, 60 n., 161–62, 184

"Ad Patrem," 164

Adam, 32, 79, 80, 81, 96, 145, 158, 175, 177, 178, 195 n., 214, 215, 217, 228, 242

Addison, Joseph, 204

Adultery, 252–53

Aeschylus, 16

Agamemnon, 12 n.

Age of Reason, The, 169 n.

Ahriman, 120 n.

Alaric, 18, 19

Alexander, 178

Ambrose, 37

Anarch, the Old, 143

Androdeism, 150

Anselm, 26, 44

Anti-Arminianisme, 67

Apollo, 12 n.

Apology for Smectymnuus, 249

Aquinas, Thomas, 99 n.

Areopagitica, 74 n., 77, 86, 87, 90, 92, 95, 99, 101, 105, 110, 116, 143, 165, 180, 184, 187, 189, 199, 200, 201, 259

Arian heresy, 27

Arians, 48, 184

Aristotelian, 172

Aristotle, 12, 13, 15, 16; Golden Mean of, 99 n., 100, 101, 103; virtues, according to, 21, 35, 36

Arminianism, 165

Arminius, Jacobus, 31, 67 n., 154 n., 161, 184, 185, 190

Arnold, Matthew, 235

Asceticism, 42

Asmodai, 178

Athanasian Creed, 28

Athanasius, 7, 35, 36 n., 38, 39, 60, 61, 139

Atonement, vicarious, doctrine of, 26, 60 n., 61

Augustinianism, 10, 17; discussion of, 17–50, 20, 21, 44, 51, 52, 54, 56 n., 76, 104

Auto de fés, 49

Bacon, Francis, 31, 33, 85 n., 164

Bacon, Roger, 51

Baconian philosophy, 5, 16

Baptists, 168

Barber, A. D., 161, 162

Basil, 36

Bay Psalm Book, The, 43

Beaux' Stratagem, 248 n.

Beëlzebub, 212, 213

Belial, 213

Bible, 4, 10, 24, 67, 178, 188

Boehme, Jacob, 119 n., 149 n.

Boëthius, 155 n.

Boulting, William, 117 n.

Bradstreet, Anne, 237

Browne, Sir Thomas, 28, 70, 149 n.

Browning, Robert, 7, 129, 139, 234, 235

269

Fludd, Robert, 119 n.
Formula of Concord, 64 n., 71
Fornication, definition of, 247
Fosdick, Harry Emerson, 188
Forsyth, P. T., 207
Free will, 24 n.
Freneau, Philip, 237

Gabriel, 215
Galileo, 110, 111, 112
Gascoigne, George, 203
Gauden, John, 166
General Spirit, 127, 128
"Genesis," 118 n.
Geneva, discipline of, 90
Gibbon, Edward, 56 n.
Gilbert, A. H., 258 n.
Gnostics, 36, 60, 118 n.
God, 4, 8, 11, 12, 13, 18, 20, 21, 25,
    26, 27, 30, 31, 32, 33, 34, 38, 40,
    41, 44, 45, 46, 49, 57, 61, 63,
    64, 65, 66, 67, 68, 69, 70, 94 n.,
    116, 117, 118 n., 122, 123, 124,
    125, 126, 127, 128, 129, 130, 131,
    132, 133, 134, 138, 139, 140, 141,
    142, 147, 148, 149, 150, 151, 152,
    153, 154, 155, 156, 157, 159,
    174, 175, 181, 184, 187, 191, 193,
    194, 195, 196, 205, 206, 207, 208,
    211, 212, 213, 216, 222, 223, 224,
    225, 231, 232, 242, 255, 263, 267
"God Glorified in Man's Depend-
    ence," 65
Godwin, William, 33, 56 n., 245
"Good Old Cause," 200
Good Works, doctrine of, 45 n.
Gospels, 25, 84, 85, 247
Goths, 18
Government, Milton's theory of,
    242
*Grace Abounding to the Chiefest of
    Sinners,* 61

Grace, universal and specific, 24 n.,
    31n., 64
Greek gods, 12
Greeks, the, 15; the arts and con-
    tributions of, 45, 47
Greenlaw, Edwin, 99 n.
Gregory of Nyssa, 36
Grisar, H., 71 n.
Guatama, 234
Gulliver's Travels, 20

Hall, Joseph, 185, 203
Hamlet, 52
Havens, R. D., 236
Heaven, 24, 32
Hebrew God, 12
Hell, 24, 115
Hellenism, 8, 9; explanation of
    term, 11–17
Henry VIII, 44
Hermogenes, 120 n.
Hero and Leander, 52
Herodotus, 7
Hesiod, 16
Hickey, Emily, 208
Hind and the Panther, The, 181
*Histriomastix: or a Scourge for all
    Stage-Players,* 67 n.
Holy Ghost, 119
Holy Spirit, 28, 40 n., 62, 64 n.,
    84, 126, 127, 127 n., 184 n., 186
"Holy Willie's Prayer," 32 n.
Homer, 7, 13, 16, 265
Horace, 18
Horton, 100, 164
Hume, David, 56 n.
Huns, 18

Iliad, The, 52
"Il Penseroso," 74, 170, 261
Immortality, 23